An Open

Relationship

Samantha Claire

ACKNOWLEDGEMENTS

This book has been a nine year process in the making and covers a period of twenty years through life's rich tapestry.

I would like to express my gratitude to the many people who saw me through this process: to all those who provided support, talked things over, read, wrote, offered comments in the editing, proofreading and design process.

I would like to thank all the people who helped me on my crowd funding campaign for enabling me to publish.

I would like to thank David Higgin, Sue Birbeck, Jennifer Manson, Davina Mackail and Lisa Ferguson for helping me birth this book in its true form. I am eternally grateful for all the hours you have all contributed to this body of work.

I want to thank Tiago and my family, who have supported and encouraged me on what has been a long, and at times difficult, journey.

I would like to thank Dominique Hazell, Sarah Nankin and Thor Selander for helping me create the visual concept for the cover.

Thank you deeply to all the beautiful people who have crossed my path – without you I would have not been able to write this book and all of you have shaped who I am today. For this I am forever grateful.

I would like to make a special thank you to Thor Selander whose belief in my work has exceeded all expectations and has been a true catalyst for getting this book out there.

"The ideal purpose of your life is that you are grateful,
great and full. That you are alive and you enjoy it."
– Yogi Bajan

To the reader...

In these changing times, many of us are finding that the conventional ways and rules of conventional relationships no longer fit us, no longer reflect what we want to express in the world.

Samantha Claire has been treading her true path of love for twenty years. Since the age of fourteen she realised that one love, one deep conversation, one focus of passion and expression was not enough for her.

In *An Open Relationship* she shares her journey through love's myriad expressions; it is a journey of growth, learning, living the full experience of life. Throughout these pages she follows the dictates of her heart, ultimately breaking through to a deep honesty, with herself, and with the people around her.

An Open Relationship is a bold, brave work. In going beyond where many would go, it shows the way to stepping back, seeing ourselves clearly, and finding our own truth on the new spectrum of love and expression.

Read it with an open heart.

All of the names in this book have been changed; each of these entries reflects the truth of a particular moment in my life. All the relationships I keep with those who have entered these pages are filled with honesty. No ties are broken.

Dedicated to all those who have touched my life.

Introduction

"Love can never possess, Love is giving Freedom to the other, Love is an unconditional gift, it is not a bargain."
– Osho

Books, journals, poems, stories, music, dance, fantasies are all attempts to create space for creation and reflection. We all have a voice inside us that needs to be heard and my sharing this journey with you comes from a deep knowing that I need to let my inner voice sing. This is the journey of a woman's sexual exploration; it is a story about love, self-discovery, honesty and the spiritual quests that unfold when one seeks to discover one's own sexual centre and truth.

This is not an easy journey; there are many conditioning systems in place that keep us from following the true desires and yearnings of our hearts. I have scars that have been buried very deep; my teenage years were spent indulging the demons that gave me a powerful sense of purpose and belonging while I was young.

This book offers a wild tangle of narratives and adventures because life is a series of fantastical voyages that weave themselves together to create a magical tapestry filled with endless jewels. The jewels are our life experiences and they in turn become the lenses though which we understand ourselves.

I hope you will take from this book what feels right for you and what resonates with you. Above all, I hope you will find what freedom means for you in your own heart.

"Freedom" is a word that is often thrown around carelessly; when truly explored it has unlimited potential and extraordinary depth. What are you willing to do to be free? What are you willing to let go of in order to have a free heart? What are you going to commit to in order to have peace? Freedom lies deep within the core of the energetic beings that we are.

I spent many years thinking freedom was something that lived outside of me; through my journey I have come to understand that freedom is a courageous exploration of the inner realm that offers us the true meaning of our lives.

I choose now to open my heart and share my life's experiences with you. In each of the following chapters you will find transcriptions from my private journals. I knew they were meant for telling a story, not for lying around gathering dust. Through these journals, my journey now reaches out to touch the hearts of strangers. I have let the angels guide me through this process to find fluidity and flow, and to find the words I need to best express my story honestly and with compassion.

I believe we are all born with an infinite abundance of love. Our birthright is that of love. As soon as we are born we encounter the systems of the outside world and so our birthright of love starts to become distorted. As we begin to interact with the systems, we grow to realise these systems, despite their intentions of growth and expansion, very much keep us from being who we need to be and from fulfilling the reason we came here.

If we look at life as a dance, the whole point of the dance is the dance. Yet we are enrolled in a system where we are taught life is about the destination; and so we arrive to life through a model of education that is all about success and achievement. We put our children into the system of schooling so they will 'become something': the lawyer, the doctor; and that becoming that 'something' will, in essence, define them.

We think that once we have ticked the boxes of high school, university, job, marriage, children, these things will make us happy; and we wake up one day, having achieved these things, to find we don't feel any different from how we felt before. We feel that space of disconnection; we stopped dancing and we missed the whole point along the way.

Life is not about the destination or journey, it is a musical thing and we were supposed to dance our way through each melody, note and tango.

The systems aim to keep us on the straight and narrow, to create order and structure and keep us from expressing our true selves.

The dance is not to let these systems define us, brand us and control us. Once we realise it's all an illusion we can move beyond them, guided by our own inner truth and wisdom, to discover the freedom and infinite possibilities that await us on the other side. We can learn to dance our own dance within the systems.

Systems are useful in order to carry out our everyday explorations; yet in many instances they are founded upon ideals that do not serve our intuitive and spiritually progressive times.

When I was younger I loved the idea of rebelling against life's institutional systems, imposing my ways and provoking reactions, because on a deeper level I understood that many of these systems lacked the fundamental structure of LOVE that is essential to any worthwhile part of life.

Very early in my life – when I was just a year old – I was diagnosed with bilateral hip displasia, which in non-medical terms means I was born with my hips out of their sockets. I spent the next two years of my life in and out of hospital with my legs in plaster of Paris. I have few memories of this. I learned to walk properly by the age of three and became a very energetic, lively little character, always on the move between this world and that. Photos reveal me as a very happy, independent, loving and playful kid. My diary entries and memories reveal another story – the story of the impact that my years in hospital had on my life. It was only in my late twenties that I was able to make sense of what happened so many years before.

My childhood was typical for a girl in any white middle-class suburban South African family: I lived with my mother and father and two younger sisters in a house with a garden, plenty of space, a car, a pool, family holidays, good government schools, after-school activities, dinners around the table each night, travels abroad. I always felt looked after and never went without anything.

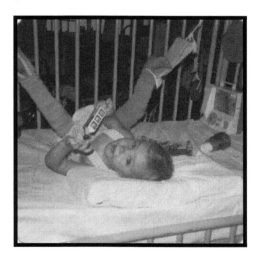

My dad was a full-time working father; my parents are South African and both my grandparents were of British stock. My mom's dad was from England, and my father spent most of his early years living six months of the year in London and six months in

Cape Town; so it wasn't a surprise to anyone when I left for London at the age of twenty to discover my place in the world.

My mom was a full-time mother until I turned twelve. Family came first for both my parents and this added to my deep sense of confidence and feeling cared for. It provided a grounding base for my childhood years. I never felt I was in need of anything. My memories are of much happiness and love.

My younger sister and I remain extremely close to each other. We lived together in London for many years and we continue to grow in our connection as sisters, mothers, close friends – both with a love for yoga and an holistic lifestyle.

There was one immense difference in our family: my middle sister Nicole has Down's syndrome. Those born with Down's syndrome are governed by three motives: food, family and unconditional love for those around them. They have a very high sex drive. From a very young age there was always an abundant flow of love, cuddles, kisses and affection in our house, and it still remains the same way to this day.

Nicole's very public display of bodily stimulation, her endless hugging of strangers and her nude stripteases were the beginning of my deconstruction of the sexual taboos that have left huge imprints in the world.

I have deep gratitude and love for my family; they have never deprived me of warmth and human touch. I have always been blessed by endless affection and loving words. I've always known that I am loved, cared for and supported. When I hear people share that they never heard their fathers or mothers say "I love you," it always leaves me feeling heartsore; I have no idea what it feels like to not be loved. The foundation that my parents created for me has felt solid and whole. It's the platform that also gave me the confidence to be able to love with an open heart.

Countless things I've done might have changed my family's affection for me – I took drugs, I crashed three cars before I was twenty-one years old, my dad walked in on me while I was having sex – the list continues. When I was sixteen I stole a large amount of money from my father. When he found out he was furious – who would blame him? His response in the following weeks was to embrace me with fatherly love. I remember his arms wrapped tightly around me and his words still echo through me: "Only when you have children will you know how easy it is to forgive."

The unconditional love I experienced growing up is the fire that fuels me to give openly, honestly and freely now in my everyday life. It has taken me many years to realise this and to free myself from the social conditioning systems that governed me for so long.

I believe it is time for a new look into who we are and who we choose to be; it's ultimately up to us to create the path we wish to follow. Yet deep within our human existence we have a system within a system, and I feel the most cunning and sly of them all is the system of lies. I was brilliant at lying; I could do it in my sleep. After we tell one lie, we always need another lie to cover it up, and the digging begins as we try to hide our truths behind tales of contrived nonsense. It was my ability to lie that has been my true teacher within this path of personal growth.

Who am I? Who are you? What is this connection we all share that makes us human, that allows us love, that allows us to travel this mysterious road? I believe it is our sexual energy that makes us connect with the people who cross our path. By sexual energy I mean the Kundalini Life Force Energy that runs through our veins, our hearts and our souls. This energy is the energy that gets us up in the morning – that allows us to feel alive, plugged in. It's our passion, it's our truth; it's in nature, and it's all around us, it's who we are. There is no separation.

This force has always been my fuel to step deeper into my sexual promiscuity and walk down the pathway of Tantra. For me Tantra is a meditative philosophy and not just about sex. It is a way of being; a method of transformation. We gain insight into the deeper meaning of Tantra when we break down and translate the Sanskrit term: TAN translates to inner self and soul and TRA translates to getting closer. Therefore TANTRA literally means getting closer to the divine soul within.

I was once reading an article and this caught my eye:

'Love is a connection. I think that connection is a culmination of many different things: empathy, compassion, lust, remembrance, recognition, cognisance, cohesion, and pheromones. Perhaps these all occur at different levels and so love occurs at different levels.'

I believe that love begins as soon as a connection is made, sexual or not. It increases as the connection becomes stronger. The only way you can prevent someone from loving is to deny that person all human contact. True unconditional love is the ability to love what is, and who each of us is. It is the hope that can transcend our differences and heal our wounded hearts and this journey of love starts with loving and healing ourselves. The more we can love ourselves, the more capable we are of really making a difference, of laying the foundations for changing our families and communities into something extraordinary.

For this reason it is my heart's calling to share my story with you. I know it is my calling to share a new way that we can live – free from sexual shame and guilt; a way we can live in integrity and honesty at the core of our being; a way to live life to the fullest in each moment that is presented to us; a way to heal past pains and traumas, let go of guilt and release the shameful conditionings that have been placed on our most sacred magical human gift – the gift of love.

Love is not something that can be boxed into one way of being, for love is infinite and goes beyond all definitions. Love is love.

For now, let's get started on a journey. Let me take you back with me to my teenage years...

Teenage Tangles

*"The meaning of Life is just to be alive. It's so plain and
so obvious and so simple. Yet everybody rushes around
in a great panic as if it were necessary to achieve
something beyond themselves"*
– Alan Watts

As the title of this chapter suggests, my teenage years were a tangle of transitions between extremes: my natural impulse to love (freely, spontaneously and passionately) and the social conditionings that made me feel "guilty" for doing so. These years taught me the meaning of honesty: my lack of it during these important years later enabled me to understand the importance of truth and the meaning of integrity in my life.

Like all teenagers, I was shifting into a new physical body; I experienced a rush of emotions, new hormones firing at different angles and a rocky rollercoaster of events, feelings, passions, lies, tears, joys and pressures.

I started my first diary journal at the beginning of high school. When I wrote these entries I was thirteen going on fourteen. I had had my first proper kiss with a boy and not a week later I was already taken with his cute friend.

8 April 1994

I think I may be in Love? I can't wait to see him at the end of the holidays. I really get afraid sometimes because I don't know if I am going to go to heaven; I know in my heart I love God and Jesus but I don't show it and don't want to go to hell. I really love you, Lord.

My early high school years were conditioned by my Christian roots; I believed that I was born a sinner, I was always repenting to God, and I always thought at the time that if something bad happened, it was my punishment for not following a righteous path.

My first little love interest was short lived; after he reached third base he lost interest. I was heartbroken. Our brief relationship only lasted a few days and when it was over he bragged to all his friends that I was an "easy girl". Soon, this name started to circulate throughout the school. Everywhere I turned I heard, "Easy girl" or "that's the one" or "she will give you a quick hand job" echoing through the halls. This was my first taste of shame.

My teenage years were spent falling in and out of love with many men and women. My first real love was my best friend, Patricia. She was beautiful; she had this angelic way about her that melted anyone in her presence. Our story began with innocent kisses on my rooftop, and before long this became a regular playtime delight. Our friendship of drunken kisses and explorations led us both to have boyfriends and our secret intimacies disappeared in the many stories that followed.

Many men found their way into my heart. Looking back, I see that each held a special place. Each relationship followed the previous one in one long chorus line – of beautiful loves, lusts, attractions, infatuations and drunken hormones, all running simultaneously in my heart. Here I'll talk about the ones who taught me love lessons and I thank them for the experiences we shared; these have made me the person I am today.

Brendon: An infatuation, an older boy filling me with desire; he was three years older than me and he wore his school uniform with a rugged style. I'd wake every day with the delight of seeing him pass me in the corridors, feeling the tingles in my chest when our eyes met. I was obsessed.

His favourite catch line was, "Call me when you turn sixteen." These words echoed with me until I was over eighteen and I finally got to share an evening with him.

"Brendon" was written on all my stationery, my books and my diary. I even fake tanned his name on my tummy one summer and when I had swimming class everyone saw his name in bold orange print and my little secret was out. Brendon occupied my time and most of it took place all within my fantasies.

My concerns about "getting a reputation" left a heavy feeling in my heart; I would walk into school and see gossip circulating the draughty corridors. As a teenager I was often sick with the flu or a cold from the constant flux of my emotions. I wanted so much to fit in, to be liked, to look good, not look bad and to love freely. I didn't want to be singled out for being "easy," but it always happened that I liked one boy after the next. I didn't know any way around the cruel gossip of teenagers and their groups.

My teenage years were spent with two amazing people Patricia and Skye. We created an amazing, unbalanced, vulnerable, loving, tangled, uncertain triangle; we did everything together. We would exclude ourselves from other groups to just hang out, the three of us. We explored a deep friendship; it was not always based on truth, but it was based on a love that we all deeply felt for each other and which saw us through our years at high school.

Next was **Jack:** He was tall with Dutch features reeling me in for the catch. He introduced me to a world of stimulating conversations, blow jobs, red wine, smoking ciggies and late night bicycle rides and he gave me a very special book, one that would always stay with me: *Journeys Out of the Body,* a book about astral travelling.

10 October 1995

I hope Jack is not using me to go far with, as I really like him. Life seems to go on and on and on and never seems to end.

I feel great today, do not know why. Only time will tell. I think

I love Jack enough that I would make love to him. I am not sure if this is going to be right, but hey people only learn from their mistakes.

7 November 1995

Hello Diary, well life is as good as can be expected, I don't have the best reputation at the moment, with SLUT AND WHORE been echoed down the corridors. Why do people make such a big deal about a few kisses? But I suppose I brought it on myself. I am still with Jack this makes me happy. I really feel I want to talk to someone, maybe God? But I doubt he would listen to a sinner like me. HELP. Another problem is that I am incredibly jealous of Patricia and Skye, I know we have a three-way friendship, but I feel terribly left out at times. I need to trust myself and know that what we each share with each other is safe and I can trust it.

Jack gave me this book called "Journeys Out of the Body". It is about Astral Travelling, when your soul leaves your body. It's so interesting; I would like to try it.

A poem

Love is something you can't touch nor hold yet you can have it inside you.

Live it, feel it and let it grow within. Love always changes. Just like Life.

It's a deep compassion between one's inner self and the world around us.

We have to love ourselves in order to be loved and give love to others.

The book Jack gave to me was so powerful, I would spend many nights practicing my breathing and allowing my soul to leave its body. It was extraordinary. Already then I was exploring consciousness.

The learnings at age 14 were already paving a way ahead for me even if I didn't understand it all then. I was already dealing with the notions of Jealousy and Shame. One way to deal with shame is to create strategies. My multiple sexual feelings always felt very natural and easy for me. I knew I was able to enjoy being attracted to more than one person. The problem was that there was no way to be honest about this with my boyfriends; I thought it was acceptable to lie or to leave things unsaid, because I was afraid of what the consequences would be otherwise. My religious beliefs held me to the idea that I would go to hell for loving more than one person, so I decided to keep all my secrets and attractions to myself.

It was also around this time that an adult figure in my social circle was cheating on her partner. I knew of the affair and that she never told her partner at the time. I decided that this was acceptable – you can have your cake and eat it too – as long as you never reveal the truth. It's only now, years later, that I am able to see things more clearly, and see the impact of what can happen when we withhold the truth.

Dave and I met at a family gathering; he carried me off on a summer romance. I experienced new tingles in places I never had before. As we lay under the hot African night sky a blanket of stars rolled our pheromones into one. Shortly after spending the summer together I booked a ticket to spend the Easter holidays with him. Our conversations started moving towards what having sex would look like;

each conversation bought me closer to my womanhood. The night I lost my virginity was very safe and loving; the backdrop was his bedroom with candles lit and Bob Marley's "Could this be Love?" playing gently in the background. I remember phoning Patricia the next morning and telling her. I felt like everyone knew my secret. I was starting my journey of sexual discovery and the path of what it means to be a woman. Shortly after Dave I met Tony.

Tony: We would sneak our time together at church youth group meetings, break times at school and we would bunk precious days out of class to enjoy and discover the passion of our connection. He made me aware of what it was like to be 'coloured' in a new South Africa. Even though apartheid is over, its residue was and still is, deeply engrained in our parents and in our cultural system.

'Coloured' might sound like a derogatory name, but in South Africa it is not considered racist – it is the name given to a large group of our population and I feel it defines South African culture. Coloured music, banter, slang, humour and dance are essential to a South African way of life.

I went with Tony to his Matric dance (like prom in the US). I felt like a princess all dressed in deep purple. He was a painter; he played guitar and roped me into the world of Uriah Heap, Jimmy Hendrix and the Doors. Our relationship came to an abrupt end when the news came that he was emigrating abroad.

3 March 1996

Music: Uriah heap
Mood: confused
Movie: "Reality bites"
Loves: Tony and Trev

Dear Diary, life is fine, I went to the carnival last night with Tony, we are going out and I really like him a lot. We drank lots of vodka shots and got very drunk. We are very passionate together, my emotional state runs away with me when we are together. I gave him a blowjob and he went down on me, he's so divine. Got home at 1.00am, when I got home Patricia and I started making out again. We have this beautiful connection and I am very attracted to her. Can't wait to finish high school and move in with Patricia and Skye. I have to stop smoking as I am running cross-country this season. I want to try LSD just to see what the feeling is like. I love astral travelling. I hope Tony doesn't tell everyone how far we went, as stuff gets around the school so fast. It's mad how people are always so interested in everyone's business.

My younger years of bisexuality felt very right for me. I rarely felt that attraction to women was something to be ashamed of. Many guys also found it quite a turn on to see girls making out at parties! I knew that women were very special; they made me feel cared for and safe and I felt deeper emotional connections with women than with men. I knew family and religion would never condone my relationships with other women, so I kept them secret and hoped that eventually I would out grow out of my bisexual "phase". I never have, although I did suppress my feelings for a number of years.

Trev was another boyfriend during my high school days. Our time was spent smoking ciggies, playing endless rounds of chess, sipping bottomless cups of coffee, going on camping trips by the sea and doing naughty things under my duvet covers. He always just seemed to be there, and when he wasn't, I would miss him. He drew beautiful pictures and taught me to play guitar. The sounds of Red Hot Chilli Peppers still transport me to fond memories of great adolescent summer days in the park.

4 November 1996

Dear Diary: Life is not going to plan. My mom found out I have been stealing money from my dad, I forgot to tell you. I am listening to Roxette and wish I could go back and be twelve-years-old when life was a bit more simple. Patricia and I had a fight; it feels strange to fight because we are also intimate with each other.

I was always stealing little bits of money from my dad; I thought I was smarter than him and that he would never know the money was missing. In the beginning it was small amounts; later it turned into larger and more frequent takings. I was also beginning to take drugs and my sense of perception was shifting radically. At the time I couldn't help myself; I felt I was entitled to the things I took. I learned again to cover the truth, and the more and more I practised, the more I realised I had a talent in pretending.

Stealing became bigger and addictive. This was also a time in my life when I was not getting along with my dad at all; we were like chalk and cheese. This doesn't excuse what I did, but it did give me a reason to continue with it. Towards the end of high school I had stolen hundreds of pounds that my dad was saving for a rainy day; if you convert the amount to Rands it was a fortune. I have carried so much guilt and shame over this, well into my late twenties and it's been such a lesson for me.

April 1997

Walking through bubbles of the past
Emotions on end, unable to comprehend
Standing still while it all passes by
A tear trickles down and splashes on the photo of all this
confusion
I make it hard
Too many strings tied
Churning me day and night
My thoughts beat out pain
No one knows any of my secrets
Can't tell
All lost
All gained
No pain no fear
I need

I want

I care

I love

I need him, them, I need me

Nathan: Another on and off love romance. He was unusual; he came from a different world of financial affluence. Wealth and fine things caught my hippie ways off-guard and I needed to explore them. We created a friendship first and spent time talking, hanging out, going away to his beach house on the ocean, playing pool, drinking good red wines and whiskeys and fine dining. For a while it worked; then, after an overseas skiing holiday, I made the mistake of bringing an English holiday romance home for a visit; Nathan broke up with me when I told him I was going to bring my English boy out to South Africa.

April 1997

It's 12pm and I must get to sleep. Lately life has become more serious, not hectically, but I really feel like I am growing up. Independence lurking around every corner. Responsibility is coming along, I taste her. It's the challenge of life ahead that I'm so excited about; I can't share it, as it doesn't contain words. I just feel different. Life is made up of tiny details. The journey is important, not the destination. Fuck that's so true, you learn and learn and learn and it never has an end. God, I feel so happy. This book is no diary, but a journal of my self.

I have joined a circus, started flying trapeze; it's amazing and I feel such a freedom when I fly.

I am trying to work out how I feel. Trapped? Longing for something? Afraid of something, always unsure. Why do I feel like this? Why do I feel so ashamed to express myself sexually? Sex drugs and rock and roll – an expression of the 60s but it's in my life, just that the music is different. I want to laugh, soar, run and fly in a single moment of life.

I thought I knew my path on the road, though there seem to be so many turns. Which one do I take? Christianity should I or shouldn't I, I know deep down it's right yet all the material things are getting in the way. I know Jesus is the way to go but I can't seem to get to his path, I have drifted away so much. I look at my Christian friends and they seem so full of life and bubbly.

May 1997

WELL I'VE JUST BEEN CAUGHT WITH DAGGA AT SCHOOL

We were called to the principal's office, the silence was unbearable. Time slowed down. We're only 16 and we could be facing a criminal record. Why can't they legalise it, they need it anyway for medicinal reasons. I have been labelled as the ringleader, how appropriate. My parents were in total shock. I have been suspended, they nearly expelled us, but thank God they didn't. My dad has me under house arrest, will only let me attend church gatherings. Praise the lord.

29th May 1997

I have given my life to the Lord, and yesterday the Holy Spirit touched me, I was talking in tongues, it was an experience I can't even begin to put into words. One moment I was outside on the fields smoking cigarettes and then the next moment I was walking slowly towards the singing coming from inside the hall. I walked down the aisle of the hall and fell to the ground in what felt like an epileptic fit, what was really happening was I was being touched by the Holy Spirit and was talking in tongues. It was magical. I feel so very different.

Looking back to that day, I feel like another presence took over my body. The feeling was one of deep soulful happiness and connectivity. I knew that I needed to shift back to my spiritual roots; part of me believed in the higher energy of Mother Earth, while other parts of me were still conditioned by years of Bible school, youth groups, and religious upbringing. The weeks that followed this new dramatic shift had me purge a lot of "evil" things. I threw out all my music, my palm reading books, anything that had the potential to draw me away from God. I do remember always having a deep sense of happiness at that time; I remember feeling such a joy and peace in my heart.

11 July 1997

What is Freedom?

Have tasted the dose of LSD – my phase with being a "happy clappy Christian" melts away as I discover a new truth. They can't judge me, they haven't done it. It opens you up and you are exposed to the real world. Noticing things that seemed so unimportant, and now seem so huge and relevant. The school is a commune of rules and rules and more of them until they tear you apart, all I want to do is be by myself. People always telling me what to do, but hey it's me in this body. I want to love it the way I want to, can't they understand? Patricia and Skye are way more than friends; they are my life support system that I learn to create from. They are family. They give me a sense of belonging and feeling safe.

From the first moment I experienced LSD, I knew things would never be the same again. I am deeply grateful for the experience it gave me; it offered a deeper awareness of self that I was looking for. I remember the morning of my first trip; I was slowly returning to that "normal headspace" when I realised that I would never return – the chemical makeup of my brain had shifted and I was different. My true questioning mind, my deeper self-awareness and my unconscious thoughts were revealing themselves to me.

I feel that my psychedelic insights were of profound importance. They opened me up to what was really happening within the universe and gave me a deeper sense of what it was I was always writing and searching for. It enabled me to deconstruct the organised religion I was so entrenched in; it allowed me to see the brainwashing and suppression of my true self that I feel religion generates on a daily basis. Although I had to go through a deep darkness during my voyage, I feel now that it was all part of a much larger tapestry of my life experience. I have no regrets.

13 September 1997

Where do I begin? At the moment life seems really amazing. On the top layer I have beautiful girlfriends, a wonderful boyfriend and great social life. It's the bottom layer that bugs me. What to think, why, how and who am I? And religion – how does it fit in? I really want the answers, the answers come from inside you and yet people seem to influence me in the way I think about life. I should do what feels right for me. God seems right, though the rules don't fit for me. Their way seems to put people into boxes so they are not able to express themselves and be themselves.

Acid has changed my life in a way I never thought possible. Decisions feel harder to make. I just want to finish high school and live my life to the fullest. After all isn't that what life is about? Yet at the moment I am stuck in this bubble of conformity, only one more year and then I can leave. I am still smoking dope nearly three years now. I want to take an acid trip again and again and again and try Ecstasy. I want to feel the rush that everyone talks about. I love Patricia and Skye so much, we are so close, we kiss, we cuddle, I can't seem to get enough of them, and they are just always there for me and I for them.

I've finally slept with Trev and it was really nice. I like him so much. Yet I have started to feel anger when I am intimate with men recently. I have started not to enjoy having my breasts touched. Where does that come from?

October 1997

This schooling thing is just not for me it does not allow us to shine as who we wish to be but rather conform us to what is expected from us. I am on the injection, so I don't fall pregnant and it makes me feel strange. Starting to notice I don't want my breasts touched? The workload is picking up and all I want to do is pop another pill, fuck Ecstasy is so incredible, it makes me feel so great, also scary cause I don't want to get caught up in the whole drug world, it's so easy to get sucked in.

As I began experimenting more with drugs, Ecstasy always seemed to be on the menu. I really enjoyed the way it made me feel, the rush that would last for hours and send tingles of love to all the cells of my body. I didn't have any awareness then about the energetic and chemical damage it was doing to my body. I was riding the waves of being a teenager and not thinking at all about what the outcomes would be.

It was December of '97 that I experienced my first wave of panic attacks. I was watching "Beverly Hills 90210" when all of a sudden I stopped breathing and everything seemed to go black, as though I was descending down a never-ending tunnel of death. I was rushed to hospital. I went through all sorts of tests to see what had caused it, but they couldn't find an answer; deep down I knew it was linked with the drugs.

The attack left me with a huge, vulnerable, open, bleeding emotional wound. I was left feeling continually anxious, like a dark shadowy creature infiltrated my everyday world. In the following months I felt like I was losing my personality; my mind and emotions had become too open. I knew I had to stop and rebuild my life. The larger panic attacks would return three more times; it took several years and my move to England to end the hold they had over me.

After that summer I was preparing to enter my final year at school. It was towards the end of that very hot and humid summer that I met a much older Englishman who introduced me to the world of cocaine. I experienced my first White Christmas. I took my first line. It felt surreal; it took away the panic I was feeling, and it filled me with a new confidence. The confidence was only temporary and soon the panic would catch up with me.

The whole thing was like a clip from a B-grade movie. Late summer was chaos: panic attacks, drug binges and a personality meltdown. Soon I was trying to clean up my act and put all the pieces of my life back together.

This was a very confusing time for me; I needed so much to feel loved, but I couldn't realise that all love begins with loving oneself. I needed to put myself first in order to begin healing. I also became far too attached to the idea of finding a 'steady boyfriend'. The summer flirting with older men and taking cocaine, mixed with my internal conflicts over past loves and old hurts, set the stage for a major internal battle within me. Yet all the while there was this overview and awareness of what I was going through. I felt my higher self knew it was meant to travel down this road and I would come out the other side.

It was also during this time that I was beginning to see how drugs and drink left me feeling unsafe and I would often wake up the morning after feeling so much shame. I would either not be able to remember the night at all, or have done stupid things in the spur of the drugged moment to be a part of the group or to just follow my wild crazy horse.

31 January 1998

VORTEX TRIP DREAM TIME (Trance festival)

(This is where I took my very last ACID Trip.)

Had the worst trip of my life. I think I am mad or going mad. HELP!!!!!!

Minds apart, fractions of mindless bodily souls, floating from one bubble to the next.

The brain doing all the movement, myself grasping the glimpse of a new insanity, a new order. I feel like I am going mad, I am only 17 years old.

Everyone laughing, I am unable to reach any point of communication and feel myself shutting down. Speech distorted, can't imagine going to school, sleep is necessary. Will I ever be able to communicate again?

We Astral Travelled through each other's spaces, three best friends and something broke. For the first time we were able to read each other's minds and what we are truly thinking. Paranoia kicks in and I can't control the evening. I freak out and my neck is stretched, back aches intensely, I feel little crystals inside my spine. I try to laugh, pretend it's not real. Ears aching and itching. Jaws clenching. Became so jealous of Patricia, I love her; I want to be with her.

You must go to bed, you have school tomorrow.

When will this feeling end, it's been more than 48 hours.

Innocence lost, need honesty, Need love, Need to make things simple... my perception of things feeling so distorted. I feel like I'm in a crazy film, the new character. I can't get out.

It was after this bad Acid Trip that my friendship with Patricia and Skye fragmented. Looking back it was such a fundamental time for me. I felt for the first time my own insanity and also a deep lack of trust. Drugs had gotten in the way of something so beautiful; and due to being so young I was not able to navigate my own thoughts in a tangible way, which allowed for so much upset and confusion to be caused.

I was also deeply involved with Patricia, yet my conditioning of not being able to be with a woman was powerful. It left with me the green lacings of jealousy, because I loved a woman and could not really tell her how I felt. This is when I started to work through and have an understanding of Jealousy and how she works. I could not project the Jealousy outwards. I had to bring it within and feel it and see what it was bringing up for me.

Rick climbed into my heart, with his extreme climbing and his dynamic crew of friends. He taught me the language of the outdoors. My days were spent on endless rock-climbing adventures, harnessed high in the sky, hiking river trails and going on countless camping adventures to try new climbing routes. I was the girl who became 'in' with all his friends. We were dangerously falling in love. It felt great to be around people who were active and full of love for the outdoors and who didn't take drugs.

Rock climbing became very healing and redeeming for me. My relationship with climbing and with Rick gave me a sense of self-worth again; I met new people, I became healthier and I connected with nature – this helped shave away the guilt, sadness and confusion I felt.

May 1998

Drugs no longer play their part. Climbing is my new drug. When you climb a pure state of ecstasy is felt, it's you and the rock.

Drum beats, the real surface to life. There is a mountain to climb, a route to walk, stones to be picked; the leaves on the trees hold knowledge. The mountain makes our destiny so true and real.

When we fall we must stand again.

We keep growing every day. We learn from everyone we come into contact with. We must be filled with a true confidence, free ourselves from aggression, pride and dishonesty. Find our madness within and love it. Write messages wherever we go. Play music, it creates happiness. Drink tea or coffee, make time for others. Paintings, we are painters of our own canvases. We must paint our own pictures with our own true understanding of what our purpose is. We mustn't hold back, we must go forth with confidence.

The greatest thing we humans need is love.

5 May 1998

Rick is lovely. I want to grow with him, but this familiar feeling has started to surface, I feel this aggression again when we are intimate. I don't wish to have my boobs touched at all. Sex feels so over rated and when we do have sex I feel so much anger move through me and not sure where to place it. Would like to be with him but not have sex. It's all so strange. Having all these feelings that overlap each other and contradict.

At this point during my teenage years, having my breasts touched (and certain other intimate moments) would unleash a rage within me. I knew this was linked to something more serious than just the physical repulsion of having my breasts touched. I decided to push these feelings aside – not having the mental stability to face whatever was causing that rage from within. I put it down to the constant change in teenage hormones and emotions. Sometimes I considered the possibility that I might have been abused. In general I hid my feelings and tried to ignore the anger.

As soon as my relationships began to grow more intimate, the rage would build up. I would either break it off or hide it. My most common trend was to be able to cheat or be with other men, as it gave me the sense that I was not going mad – that I was still attracted to another – and it allowed me to hide all the emotional anxiety and confusion I was experiencing and trying to make sense of.

Christmas 1998

My dad caught me having sex. Fuck. This is so hectic. I was on top and about to have an orgasm when all of a sudden I look up and see my dad, my curtain had fallen down and I think I was making too much noise and I had had too much to drink.

When my father saw me some part of him shifted. His notion of me as a little girl fell away and he was left with a space, which then filled with anger and disappointment. It was another moment of truth – the truth that I was sexually active and becoming a woman. I was no longer his little girl. He didn't talk to me for what felt like months. I don't blame him; he needed time to process what he saw. I "learned" that I needed to be more secretive and careful.

Today I try withhold nothing, even if it makes things uncomfortable, but at seventeen I was too emotionally confused to even contemplate an honest relationship with my father.

I had finally finished high school and was going to study Acting for Film and Television.

The Crash

Looking back at all the hormones, drugs, awakenings, boys, girls, highs and lows, I see the theme of love emerging time and again during my teenage years. My need to be loved reverberates throughout all my journal entries. My body and mind would undergo the chemical changes that happen when you fall in love – butterflies in the stomach, extreme happiness and abundant sexual energy – and I would find myself feeling happy about everything.

The rush was exhilarating; each new gamble offered the possibility of an exciting treasure to be found. I was so enthralled with each new relationship that I readily jumped into each game of love with the same enthusiasm as the last. I played this game, continuing to fall in love again and again. My openness to share love with others attracted all sorts of delightful and strange characters along the way. I felt like I could have whomever I pleased, and this gave me a sense of immense confidence.

Much of this "game of love" was focused on fuelling my ego. I mean of course, my unhealthy ego, the one that fills us with a false perception of power, security and certainty. Falling in love fed my ego; it made me feel I was wanted, liked, adored, popular, in demand and powerful. On the inside, however, I was frightened, confused and unable to communicate the true and honest multiplicity of my affections. I had no model for how multiple relationships or multiple loves might work in a healthy way, so I was left with cheating and playing games.

My teenage years also sowed the seed of realising that something sinister had happened in my earlier years. It was not until my early thirties that I was able to make sense of the upsets and traumas that can be so deeply rooted in one's past.

I have always been fascinated with the sexual connections and chemistries between people and as I moved into my first year at college my games became more real, mad, sad, terrifying and electrifying. I knew from a young age that I wanted to be an actress. I wanted to go to Hollywood and be famous – simple as that. During my last year of school I went for a theatre interview at City Varsity and I was accepted immediately. It was a great feeling. Throughout my school years I had never been an academic and with my dyslexia my internal dialogue ran like this: 'I am stupid and not clever enough' – so to be accepted to college based on an audition gave me a sense of purpose and inner clarity.

My father paid for my studies, as is the case with most middle class South African families. I had the option to take a year off and go to London but I decided to study and I'm thankful that I did. My London adventure would come a few years later.

City Varsity wasn't far from home; it was only a thirty-minute drive to where my classes were taught, nestled right under the magnificent setting of Table Mountain herself.

It was a huge jump from my familiar school routine and lifestyle. I could wake up late, drive my own car to campus, drink coffee; wearing everyday clothes gave me a great sense of self expression – five years of conformity and wearing a red and white checked dishcloth uniform can take creativity from you – and I could go out at night (every night if I wished). I loved my new independence, driving, my new social life, and I began to step into a new pair of shoes –

acting shoes.

I walked into my classroom – an expanded attic space full of strangely dressed thespians – and I knew immediately that the next two years would be different from what I had thought drama school would be. I thought being an aspiring actress would involve arriving fashionably late, hanging out on film sets, reading plenty of theory, watching movies and drinking bottomless cups of coffee. The coffee part I got spot on, the rest turned out to be quite different and I needed to learn fast if I wanted to become the famous actress of my dreams.

My two years of college brought endless self-development; I needed to deconstruct my old self in order to make space for a new me. There were movement classes, self analysis, voice classes, monologues, rehearsals, role plays, experiments in boundary setting and painful workshops where we endured harsh criticism in the hope of gaining a deeper understanding of ourselves. In my case these usually ended in tears and added additional layers of panic to my already anxious mind.

I learned that acting is more about getting to know yourself than becoming a famous artist. In that weird and wonderful attic my questioning mind began to explore, play, act, scream, dance, cry, talk, debate, share, touch and grow. It was in this room that I began to make baby steps towards the freedom I was searching for. I began to feel like I belonged, that I was accepted, that I was a creative being. In school I felt I never fitted in – I was always the outsider, the one in trouble. My varsity days gave me the foundation of freedom to be who I wanted to be, dress how I wanted to dress and to be a part of a group of people who all wanted the same thing. It was exciting; we didn't know what the outcome would be. The adventures we went on sent my head spinning. I loved the buzz.

I took a seat on the floor and the sound of my new, imposing lecturer's deep Afrikaans accent soaked deep into my awareness. He gave us three cardinal rules for surviving the next two years:

Acting is not for sissies (meaning it was not for the meek and mild or faint-hearted)

Always arrive on time (time is money in the film game) and

Don't screw the crew. The last rule I vetoed immediately. Even as I dropped my gaze, a beautiful row of men sat before me. I was in heaven. Who was going to be my first catch?

In the two years that followed I continued to explore my bisexual tendencies. I found myself making love to beautiful lesbians, many of them years older than me. Some of them made piles of money and wined and dined me on the way to lovemaking.

During this time, I again began to feel uncomfortable with having my breasts touched. I experienced volcanoes of rage and it was only in the arms of women that I felt calm and safe. I kept these feelings to myself. I didn't want to let "the boob issue" get in the way of working through the list of fellow thespians and bar staff I wanted to experience.

So I let myself be uncomfortable and I acted like nothing was wrong. I was having the ride of my life; I moved out of home and crashed on the floor of a dodgy house next to where I worked at the Rolling Stones pool bar. I rode all the ups, downs, sharp bends, circles, backstreets and zebra crossings of my life, not paying any attention to the stop signs or red robots (the South African term for traffic lights). I had already crashed two cars at this point.

In these college journals I was pushing myself deeper into every role, every character and every script that was given to me. I was determined to succeed as an actress. The first feedback I ever received in class went something like this: "Samantha, you are like a wild horse galloping through every terrain and never stopping for a pause; you need to tame the horse and make her still." This perfectly reflected my life outside the attic windows; I was seizing every moment with heartfelt passion and extreme play, even if this caused many hearts to cry, including my own.

Hearing my teacher's voice now, I think that this was the most valuable piece of advice anyone has ever given me. I have always felt like a wild horse with too much energy and I've never known how to quiet my mind and soul. Back then I was full of energy; I was always on the move from one thing to another, from one thought to the next, from one idea to the other, and from one lover to the next. Some people thought that I had ADHD (Attention Deficit Hyperactivity Disorder), but I was never diagnosed with having it. I was written off as a naughty dyslexic troublemaker. My sense is that my excessive energy originated from my earliest days, being stuck in the hospital; I only learned to walk much later. My young little self never got to run around like a normal one or two-year-old. I spent day after day with my hips in plaster of Paris and I had so much unchannelled energy. Acting was the first of many things to help channel that energy – so in many ways my lecturer was right: I was a wild horse who needed to find her stillness. But college wasn't my time to be still; I needed to ride the terrain.

February 1999

I am only eighteen and I have already slept with 26 people. Why can't I be normal? I am not a nymphomaniac but I love being attracted to people and kissing them, it's like a challenge. But in the process I am fucking myself emotionally 'cause I make bonds to all of them. I'm left at the end of the day scared, vulnerable and insecure. I so need their connection and love. I have to win their affection. Why do I need to be wanted?

This need to feel validated through intimacy started to break my horizon. I knew that I was playing with fire, I knew then that something was out of alignment with my higher self, yet didn't know how to express it all, how to share my vulnerability of being me. So instead I did what a lot of people do, I became stronger in my masculine self and shut down the part of me that really wanted to be expressed.

4 March 1999

Sitting in the comic space of my new film world. So many different characters pop in and out. People chattering, voices mingling, clouds of smoke, hands expressing, minds consuming, worlds confronting, mannerisms telling stories, hands writing, eyes crying with all sorts of untold stories

So many people have crossed my path; we eat, we kiss, we chat, we finger, we fuck, we play, I cry and we all smoke the same cigarettes. Had a one-night stand last night and I know that I was just used for sex. Drunken and distorted nights created a fake happiness, bringing us together through touch and meaningless chatter. Why would I do that to myself? Why would I have sex with someone when I didn't actually want to?

I had numerous moments of intimacy with guys from my college. Awkward days followed. Mostly I played around when I was drunk or high. I was still socially drinking and I had started using cocaine again. I first tried cocaine in the summer of 1997, the "White Christmas" I mentioned earlier. I enjoyed it because it allowed me to escape my panic attacks. I later dated a guy who was a regular user and who took me deeper into this world. The film world that I was starting to enter was also riddled with white fluffy bags of confidence. I liked it, but I knew I had to be careful – I had a personality predisposed to addiction. My relationship with cocaine ended several years later, after I had moved to London.

A lot of my sexual experiences were under the influence of alcohol or drugs and looking back I see how damaging this was, as it created unsafe spaces for connection and intimacy. Most of the attractions were fuelled when under the influence and then the next morning would come. Having given my power away the night before, I would have to build my self-esteem up from scratch again.

My relationship with Patricia and Skye shifted after I started Varsity. We would see each other from time to time, but our new friends and new schedules left little time for our magical three-way connections to be restored and renewed. Our friendship was still healing from the split that had happened after our acid trip.

July 1999

Men pop in and out of my life and part of me just watches and lets it happen. I need stability – one man to care for. I have slept with 6 people this year and have walked away with nothing but a broken heart.

That December I went on a skiing trip with my family to Austria. Austria was beautiful, and it was the first time I had seen snow. It was a magical ten days of a winter wonderland fairytale.

Every fairytale has a dashing Prince and mine was an English carpenter named **Mark**, on holiday with his parents. He captured my heart that winter. We spent nights dancing to remixes of 70s music and drinking endless fugals (Red Bull and red vodka) that kept us buzzing all night long. We shared slippery ice kisses and spent our afternoons hanging out watching MTV.

Before the end of my trip, Mark and I had exchanged numbers, and we decided that I would go and spend a week with him in his hometown, just outside Oxford. I was thrilled.

I said goodbye to my parents in Vienna and set out to travel alone through Amsterdam and England. My father, who helped fund my travels, made this all possible. I remember crying on my first night in Vienna. I was in a lonesome little room in the hotel 'Mozart.' It was the first time in my life I had been on my own and I was overwhelmed by the endless possibilities that lay outside the door. All I could do was let my tears soak the pillows of the little single bed I slept in.

After three days in Vienna I took a train to Amsterdam; the train was late and by the time I reached Grand Central it was one o'clock in the morning. I was tired, in a new place with nowhere to stay, and I was a touch anxious. It was then that I met a beautiful Australian man who offered me a place to stay for the week. My thoughts ran wild at his offer: "But he could be a serial killer", "You don't even know him", "He could drug you and rape you", "My dad would have an absolute fit!" Of course, my answer was: "Sure I would love to stay with you."

I still think of Amsterdam as the place where I had my first real experience of freedom. There was no one to tell me where to go, what to do, what to eat, what time to wake up or what I should say. I trusted my feelings and followed Stuart to his apartment. It ended up being a very good choice.

The days to follow were full of juicy Dutch life: the Van Gogh museum, joints in Wondel Park and cycling the city at night. The canals glisten with poetic life, the bars and clubs hold an extraordinary energy and the red light district hosts very young, beautiful women standing in windows with red neon lights dancing behind them, selling seduction. It was all such an eye opener for a young nineteen-year-old-from-South-Africa girl.

Stuart and I developed a crush on each other. He knew I was to meet Mark in London so we kept it simple and just kissed from time to time. He looked after me very well and we formed a comfortable and loving friendship that would last for many seasons.

I said my farewells to Amsterdam and I made my way to the United Kingdom. Before I joined Mark, I arranged to spend a few days in London. Earl's Court was my hunting ground; I drank pints, played Jenga, stole kisses in bars and dorm rooms and met up with fellow South Africans, Kiwis and Aussies. Finally, I made my way to Mark.

A strange romance unfolded between the two of us. Was it love? A disaster? Fate? Lust? In the end, I think it was all of these things. I wasn't able to see at first that we couldn't have been more different; we drank so much alcohol to find our common ground that I struggled to keep up with him. A sober day would arrive and he wouldn't know how to be affectionate, caring or loving. Put a few pints down him in the evening and it was a completely different story.

I was still very infatuated with him so I let myself be taken along for what felt like the ride of my life. The week went by quickly and after seven sleepless nights I found myself standing on a departure platform waiting to board my train and make my way back to South Africa, as it was my last year at University..

The next two months were beautiful and strange. I slipped back into my old life as though nothing had happened, but my heart was sore and confused Then, just before Easter, I got a call from Mark saying he had booked his ticket to South Africa and that he was dying to see me. Without fully thinking this through, I agreed to his visit, knowing full well that the relationship was based on sex and alcohol and not on any point of true connection.

Mark brought with him the cold, chilly remains of winter. Hours after he arrived things shattered and melted beneath my feet. The first two hours were wonderful – we were happy to see each other again, and we had passionate sex. I thought things would be okay. "I have this man in my country for two weeks," I thought to myself, "this will be fun." The second day everything went flying helter skelter, literally!

It was early in the evening and we had had a few drinks at a lovely restaurant on the water's edge. After we finished we loaded into the car. My sister, Leigh, was the front passenger, Mark was in the back and I was designated driver. I was driving up the hill towards the highway when Leigh turned up the volume to a favourite song that reminded the three of us of our crazy time in Austria: *"you and me baby aren't nothing but mammals, so let's do It like they do on the discovery channel."* In the moments that followed, time seemed to slow down and distort. When I recovered, I realised I had somehow crashed the car going uphill and rolled it four times in the rain. Leigh was flung halfway out the window and Mark was trying to get me out of the car in case of a fire or explosion. I couldn't bear to look at Leigh as we tended her wounds. Her kneecap was ripped off and I knew that I would have to make that dreadful phone call to my parents who were holidaying a couple of hours away and tell them the story. The ambulance arrived, with good South African timing, half an hour after the tow truck. They took Leigh to surgery. The car was a write off. It was Mark's second day and we were all in hospital in such shock and upset.

This was my third accident. I wanted to run as far away as possible from all the mayhem but the universe wanted me to face it all head on. And that's what I had to do. I had to face it and learn from it.

Leigh was in plaster. She would be healing for a good six months. Mark's affection melted away the minute the windshield smashed. The following two weeks were a total nightmare. His cold silence made me uncomfortable in my own house.

The accident provided me with a real wake-up call about pushing things too far. I had to take responsibility, stop drinking and driving and stop telling lies. Lies gather momentum and energy, and the more we tell them, the more they weigh us down physically and emotionally. I believe that all the lies up to this point had manifested themselves in the form of this car crash.

The crash also made me face the ugliness of death; there was a moment when my sister could have died and this led me to dig deeper into my spiritual voyage and to begin considering things in a brand new light.

AN OPEN RELATIONSHIP

Learning a new Language

With Easter gently passing and Leigh healing, things gradually started to return to normal. I was in a quiet place after the accident; I found myself reflecting on what I wanted from life and relationships. I was looking for a way to hold things together, to ground myself, to find a way to settle my mind and my soul. I was also ready to turn away from the rush of falling in love and discover a way to love to myself.

Hendrick was a boy who was in my drama class and from the first day of college we had never clicked. We didn't like each other at all. His background was Afrikaans and I felt he came from another time and place; in my mind he was just a simple farm boy.

I couldn't have been more wrong. Hendrick became the catalyst for my spiritual evolution. He led me down the path toward learning a new language of love. To this day we remain the very closest and dearest of friends.

The wind pounded the air. I found myself sitting with Hendrick in a cosy steakhouse eating smoked snails in garlic sauce and feasting on stimulating conversation. Our words to each other landed with such clarity and depth. I connected with him without things needing to be sexual; it was the start of a beautiful new awakening. My relationship with Hendrick was an angelic experience of loving someone without the need for sexual intercourse or sexual play.

It was wonderful to be laughing with someone, being silly and real and making animal noises. Taking walks on the beach, cuddling and snuggling until noon. Our dreams magically weaved our days into nights; we shared fancy dinners, smoothie breakfast mornings, sunrise meditations on the beach and coffee bursts that sent us into never-ending bliss. I was falling in love for real.

I had stopped drinking and taking drugs and in the months that followed I was in a very healthy state. I was starting my healing journey; becoming aware of the value of metaphysical healing, fortune-tellers, past life regression, reiki, naturopaths, colonic hydrotherapy, meditation, yoga and nature. I so enjoyed the organic flow of love with Hendrick. Deep within I felt seeds of happiness beginning to sprout.

I began to understand what loving myself could feel like. I learned that the language we use to describe ourselves and others can take away our power and I started actively speaking and seeking light and truth. I examined how past actions and injuries can pave the way for a future that mirrors the past, unless we choose to see the future as a new and open canvas and let go of old wounds. I explored what taking drugs meant for me. If I was to truly love myself, I needed to avoid things that didn't serve me.

It was also during this time that I accumulated numerous injuries related to my ankles. I was always rolling over on my ankles, which had caused the ligaments to tear. Mostly it was during the nights of drink and drugs that I would injure myself.

16 July 2000

My birthday – it is a new time for me, new people, new interests, new conversations; I have been waiting for this.

Finally I am at a level at which I get stimulated. A beautiful boy – I think he is my soul mate – is feeding and nourishing my newly found path. At times I doubt, but I place faith in those hands and lap up all the moments we share together.

A new way of life; I feel good, no drugs and no booze and there are people who respect me. I just want to be happy. My past is slipping away, replaced with kindred feeling. The past is the past and the future is whatever I wish it to be. It is going to be bright, with many colours, and full of lush moments.

Am I falling in love? He is so different, in touch with his feminine side, he holds me close and I feel loved. Maybe one day we will make love but for now, holding hands and small kisses are electrifying enough for me. He makes me laugh with all my senses.

I am sick at the way lust can rule over one, how it has caught me in its web time and again. Right now I am learning a new language, a language of loving without it having it be sexual. I am very attracted by him; he doesn't seem to make any advances. It's better that way.

Back then lust allowed me to enter situations that I may not have entered otherwise. I was often under the influence of something, even if it was just a few glasses of red wine. I didn't have the discernment to follow my true heart's yearning. I'd always take the lustful route and let my short-lived experiences fuel up my love tank. Looking back, though, I was never full; I always wanted more, something deeper and something lasting.

The flow of love is always around us. It is important to let our hearts guide us and be open to fully receive. Sometimes this takes the form of lust; there is nothing wrong with this. It is important, though, to ask ourselves clear questions: Will this moment fulfil me? Am I awake? Are all parties involved acting from a space of love to enrich each other's experience? Will this connection enable a person's "love tank" to reach its full capacity? Will this moment bring us deeper into our divine purpose?

Lust has its place, and it is important to know this place and to acknowledge it. Love, on the other hand, needs to be shared all of the time – there is never an inappropriate time for love. Love is what makes our experience on Earth so joyful and magical. In my experience, once lust was played out it left me feeling low and drained of vital energy. Love, however, keeps on growing and growing, and it brings great transformations.

Hendrick and I grew very close in the months leading up to November. He allowed me to breathe and I was able to be myself; I cared for him in a way I hadn't experienced before. I felt I could truly be myself with him; I didn't have those weird sex moments. When I wasn't in the mood, I could still cuddle up and still get my daily dose of loving. This was also a time for me to recover from the rage I felt when my breasts were touched by other men and encounters. Hendrick allowed me to feel safe.

2 November 2000

My varsity days are coming to an end in just over two months; so much has shifted for me. I am surrounded by these beautiful faces that I have been close to every day from 8am-9pm, 6 days a week for two years. We are like a family. I am sad that Hendrick didn't finish out the drama course, but he needs to follow his path as a healer. I have learned so much about myself the past two years. Hendrick is going to London next year and I know I am going to miss him so much.

City Varsity facilitated my voyage to embracing my true passion for dance and movement. My experience there allowed me to see that I didn't want to be another famous Hollywood superstar. It awakened in me the need to continue my studies in Physical Theatre. I was offered a place in a physical theatre company called the Focal Joint and I felt motivated to follow my dream of becoming a performer in dance and theatre. I didn't know then that London was in my cards.

8 November 2000

Have started getting regular shiatsu treatments and it's amazing how deep I am going into the relationship between emotions and the body, it's all linked. We are working a lot on my liver, which is related to anger. I feel this is the anger I have been ignoring for so long, the anger that is related to the feelings I have about my breasts being touched, my feelings about intimacy. I don't know where to take this investigation or how it's all linked yet I know that it's related to my past. I have faith that I will be able to link the dots and am thankful for Hendrick who opened this path up for me.

Faith was a word I would have always linked to my

Christian days, but I was beginning to understand faith in a new light. I began to regard faith as a devotion to oneself and to the Universe, not to the God that I had always been taught to fear. I was starting to see how programming and conditioning steer the course of contemporary society. It was everywhere: religion, parenting techniques, school systems, compulsory monogamous relationships, a million systems telling us what is proper and what is not.

These systems don't wish for us to speak from the heart, to sing our joys, to dance our tribal dances on the sidewalk, to hug strangers, to share our money, to kiss our friends, to get to know our neighbours, to dress in bright and outrageous clothing, to walk around naked, to be late for meetings, to speak our heart's message of love, to make too much noise, to laugh for no reason, to school our own kids, to say no to the TV screens, or to be in loving relationships. No, the job of such systems is to keep us in line so that we don't have chaos and so that we don't override anything that holds our social structures in place.

I was sick of being part of the system. I wanted another way around it. I wanted to run free and to learn the art of being happy.

15 November 2000

So many decisions to make: What shall I do next year? Go to Colorado to do physical theatre? Go travelling? Stay in South Africa and make it? Every day I have a different country in mind.

Hendrick and I are growing so close; we had such a superb night last night. We drank ourselves drunk with Oreo milkshakes and cheesecake. Lay with him naked last night for the first time, or should I say half-naked, my breasts on his chest, I know that he and I are destined for something. What? I don't know yet.

28 November 2000

REALISATIONS

A lot happened last night. I went to the beach for drinks with friends and had a little too much to drink. I hate feeling like that. Went past the bar where I used to work and meet a new friend, who is much older than me, who is practiced in the art of tantra. We chatted for long time and then the inevitable happened, we shagged, although this time it was different, it was the first time I have had a spiritual connection linked with sex. Then it dawned on me: I don't actually like sex, I mean I have never had a full body orgasm at this level until this point and to be honest I haven't found the actual act of sex enjoyable. It was strange. He showed me another side to myself. Can't tell Hendrick, he will be so hurt.

All the sex I had experienced up to this point had been fun yet I had never been able to experience full feminine ejaculation and oneness of self. This one night stand was the first time I experienced this and it was very moving for me.

Grant was practiced in the art of tantra. Tantra is an ancient yet simple meditation science that gives one access to a deeper understanding of oneself; it allows one to fully explore all six senses and to find the intimacy, sexual fulfilment and loving spiritual energy that is every human's birthright.

That night we sat naked in lotus position, locked eyes and allowed our breathing to synchronise. After about thirty minutes of silent eye gazing, he held me and made love to me; we never lost eye contact once the entire time. The whole experience left me tingling for hours after. My past encounters with sex had mostly left me feeling as though there was something missing, that I was dirty, that there was something I was not getting. Most of my sexual adventures had been full of fleeting moments of lust and passion. I found then that I wanted something deeper, a soulful connection that would break me through into enlightenment.

I continued searching for this late into my twenties, and it wasn't until I was in my thirties that I was able to really journey deep into the depth of orgasm, and into the powerful magic that occurs when sex becomes a bridge for healing and profound union of oneness.

After I graduated I was excited to start working and make some money of my own. Until this point I had always relied on my dad for support; he was happy to help but in my heart I knew I wanted to be self-reliant. After I graduated I got a job as an au-pair. I struggled to find acting work and in all my auditions I found myself alongside super-tall, skinny, size six models (nowadays it's a size zero). It was a very transitional time. I was flicking through the internet looking for courses to do in London in Physical Theatre, as I had decided to go to London to be with Hendrick, yet at the same time I wanted to create my own space and my own reasons for going. I decided to do my Masters in Physical Theatre, studying the Jacque Lecoq Method.

February 2001

One thing that I am learning fast is the need for honesty; the more I am honest the more I feel like myself. The only person I can rely on is me; I have been enjoying spending time with me. Everything that has happened has done so for a reason.

The girls I look after teach me so much about my conditioning and how language plays such a vital role in how we communicate with others. For example the word NO – I use it far too often, and instead of talking through and creating choices with them, I often catch myself saying No. I am practicing this new conversation with them and myself.

As I looked after the kids aged six and three, I practised what I had learned in my Louise Hay course. I tried to use positive language and I looked for alternatives to the word 'No'. I also allowed them to take their time to learn things and to find their own way. I was practising leading from an open heart and applying this new language that Hendrick had opened up for me.

My first workshop I ever did on this path of self discovery was called *Learning to Love Yourself* by Louise Hay. Louise Hay is a remarkable woman who healed herself from Cancer. The short version of her story is that doctors found a huge growth on her ovaries and said she needed an operation. Instead of going down the conventional route she used alternative and metaphysical healing to transform her life and her health. She discovered during this time that the damage in her ovaries was linked to childhood sexual abuse that she had blocked out of her memory. As she continued her healing work, she soon began to experience positive results and a few months later her tumour disappeared. Her story is inspirational; she is one of many remarkable individuals who have chosen to take personal healing into their own hands. She has been one of the key figures to inspire me on this path of healing and deep inquiry.

The work I accomplished during the course enabled me to transition onto my new path with strength and determination. It showed me that living honestly created energetic lightness and anxiety-free head spaces. It showed me that my lying had to stop. It reminded me that in order to find flow and joy in life we need to speak the language of the heart. This is what I was beginning to really understand – that the language of the open heart can guide us, and with it we can create anything we want in our lives.

The course helped me become more conscious of my own thoughts and of the negative language we often use to describe others and ourselves. For the first time, I was able to fully grasp that I am the creator of my own life. The exercises we did offered practical ways to look deeper into our hearts and find the hidden delights of our own divinity.

One of the exercises that really moved me the most was a mirror exercise. We had to look into our mirrors and affirm three times in a strong and passionate voice that we loved ourselves. 'I love you Samantha, I love you Samantha, I love you Samantha.' I cried on the third 'I love you' as I realised that up until that moment I had only known how to love myself on an intellectual level. I realised that I needed to experience from the depths of my heart and soul that I truly loved myself. It also brought up my lack of self love and that there was a deep trauma hidden somewhere in my past. I still didn't have the courage to go there. It felt very blurred to me so I pushed it back and worked with the concrete things that I could manage and see in my life.

The course left me with a new foundation to start walking the path of honesty, self-love, acceptance and compassion. It would take another seven years for me to really begin to live by those principles in my everyday life. I was beginning to see the deep importance of honesty and I was starting to try it out from time to time.

When I was honest I noticed how light I felt. My honesty, however, only occurred in short spurts, and it wasn't consistent by any means. I was still very selective about saying what I thought would be nice to hear, and withholding what I thought would be too confrontational for others. I was afraid of looking bad. My commitment to honesty only came much later, when I had gone through enough to be able to step into my seat of power and responsibility.

27 June 2001

In a month a new city awaits me, with new bio-rhythms, new people, new voices, new sounds, new smells, new places, new tastes, new sights. I feel like I am in a fairytale. I miss him so much. I can't wait to be with him.

I am ready to be with him in whatever way it looks. I received a letter from Hendrick that really upset me, but I wasn't shocked, he said was unable to give me what I wanted on a physical level. I am still going to go over and stay with him, as I know we share something special; maybe he will grow to become attracted to me. I am leaving the whole thing open to whatever gets played out.

The reaction I felt from reading Hendrick's letter was sadness; I was sad that he did not want to be with me in a more intimate way. That being said, the letter didn't surprise me; I had suspected it for some time, given our lack of sexual play. Despite the rejection I felt, I knew we had something magical together and in the most hidden corners of my heart I secretly hoped that I could change his sexual preference, or that he could be with me and have his boyfriends, too.

June 2001

I have just started reading "Conversations With God" by Neale Donald Walsch, The Little Girl I look after said something so profound to me and she is only 6 years of age. She said "can you see all the particles in the air? now God is made from all the air particles" she calls it love particles that collect together and make energy. Wish I could see them! Amazing, kids are filled with such magic.

Conversations with God is still high on my list when it comes to great books about developing self-awareness. It resonated with me and it allowed me to accept my Christian upbringing and at the same time to grow beyond the rules, fears and indoctrinations of Christianity. It allowed me to understand "God" as something all around, within, and beyond us. People use many words and concepts, such as chi, energy, kundalini, yin yang, Holy Spirit, divine presence, Mother Earth and Gaia to express their sense of this larger presence. The book seemed to respond to all the questions that I had been silently asking myself for years. All the passages in the book touched me deeply and they gave me a fresh way to look at love and faith, life and death, good and evil. It helped me overcome the guilt I was carrying for not choosing to be a Christian, and it gave me the confidence to walk the new path I was just beginning to explore.

With my departure for London imminent I felt prepared to

leave behind an old me. I was ready for a new change of pace; new rhythms, people and cultures. I was eager to get lost again and jump heart-first into all that life could throw my way. My days at college had opened me up. I had found the career path that I wished to walk. This gave me a deep sense of confidence to pursue what I loved and that was Movement and Acting.

By the time I left for London, I was beginning to take responsibility for most of my choices and I knew that I couldn't blame anyone for my actions anymore. I had the power to choose all that I wanted. Honesty was beginning to take root in my life, although I still struggled to share the deep truths within and the endless list of men and women in my life. The cheating still continued, love triangles and tangles still weaved themselves into my new London life and when it came to being really honest with my partners, I wasn't always able to tell the whole truth – I would often make things look as pretty as possible and withhold important things in order to stay in the game.

Hendrick opened a whole world of possibility and wonder. I had only just started to learn this new language of expression, and still to this day I have to remind myself to speak from the heart and speak my truth. Some days we are caught in our everyday habits and we forget to stay open and connected to the source of love and honesty.

It was amazing the newness and lightness I felt as I finally found a spiritual path that resonated with me. I knew it was just the beginning and in my heart I made the commitment to always stay connected to this path, however hard or however challenging it might get.

I was ready with such excitement for London's calling, ready to shed my old skin, shake up the tempo and start dancing.

> *'Dance like no one is watching and*
> *love like you have never been hurt '*
> *– William Purkey*

AN OPEN RELATIONSHIP

The Wave

I arrived in London. The cold wind brushed over me as I stepped off the plane and the icy cold smell of London carried a familiarity from my previous short visit. A new game awaited me beyond Heathrow's doors, a journey I never expected. To this day the city brings me a rich assortment of people, experiences, loves, tears, joys, food, accents, meetings, shamanic quests, travels and a wonderful soul family and community. This was the beginning of my search for peace within my noisy head, my racing heart and my wild, free and loving spirit.

When I reflect on my journey though London, I think of five previous relationships. My London story is a dance; a series of waves crashing from one shore to the next, from one relationship to another. Within each wave I discovered insights, learnings and healing. Each relationship brought me one step closer to loving myself and one step closer to understanding what had happened to me so many years ago in hospital.

My journey through London is closely linked to the ecstatic dance meditation I practise called *The Five Rhythms*, from Gabriel Roth; the five phases of the dance are "flowing", "staccato", "chaos", "lyrical" and "stillness". These rhythms reflect our everyday lives of coming and going, eating and sleeping, working and playing, doing and being. I have been dancing my whole life, though I only connected with The Five Rhythms when I was twenty-four years old in London.

The Five Rhythms mirror states of being; they are a map of everywhere you travel in your life. The dance itself is open to anyone of any age and body mass. It is a wonderful way to achieve ecstatic kundalini energy flow within your body. The rhythms explore various layers of the self and they teach us about achieving presence within and getting out of our noisy heads.

Why dance? In dancing, you can track memories and you can find gestures and shapes that help you tap into your instincts and intuitions. The Five Rhythms reveal ways that you can creatively express anger, vulnerability, joy, anxiety, sadness and ecstasy. They unleash the full potential of our bodies' movements to create dynamic healing and transformation.

> *"Put the Psyche in motion and it will heal itself."*
> *– Gabriel Roth*

Hendrick picked me up from the airport. I was staying with him at his friends until we found a place of our own. I still hoped deep down that he might be heterosexual and that I could be the one to change him. I let myself be carried away by my own fabricated fairytale romance. I had three months to explore London before my intense postgraduate studies started that October.

My feelings were all over the place; I was in a new city and I loved the newness and the zesty nightlife of Soho. Hendrick knew my tales; he didn't mind me sharing my attractions and crushes. After all, he was gay and women can tell anything to their gay boyfriends. Only with Hendrick it was all a little too close to home; we were still sharing a double bed, cuddling, kissing and taking baths and I knew I wanted more.

Three days after I arrived, Hendrick got us special passes

and took me to Stonehenge for my 21st Birthday. We left early in the morning, to see the sunrise and touch the stones. It was a magical gift.

July 16 2001

Stonehenge

The beginning of a new millennium, my birthday, with my soulmate. Here I am on my third day of my new adventure and I am at Stonehenge. It is so calm. Here I am touching the rocks and I feel a deep sense of clarity. I feel I understand God's love and freedom. I know we have a choice to create our lives as we wish. I have a few weeks before my course starts and I really need to root myself in the rhythm of England.

Sitting here, my socks damp from the morning dew, my tummy folds roll over my jeans. I feel alive.

I was enjoying having Hendrick so close while still having my freedom to date and kiss others. Being with Hendrick during this time allowed me to experience him on a new level and left a lot of room for us to grow, laugh, cry, cuddle, share, be close and love each other. The only thing it didn't permit was for us to make love; I was OK with this, although at times it frustrated me and deep down I wanted more from him.

There was a lot of tension for me at this time about either embracing or restricting my sexuality; the same was true concerning my relationship with drugs and alcohol. I could see that when I did drink, I would act in a way that made me feel awful in the morning, as though all my integrity had slipped through the window. Alcohol also released my sexual appetite and opened the way for another crush, another kiss, another shag or another one night stand. I saw this but I still didn't know how to break the cycle.

At this point my views on love and jealousy were still being shaped. I wasn't jealous in the sense that I didn't want Hendrick to be with another man. I was more upset because I couldn't get him to want me like he wanted a man. I felt insecure – like something was wrong with me. I didn't mind him being with guys; I just wanted him to desire me as well.

My anxiety attacks were still a problem at times, and they came at the most inappropriate moments, when I really needed to be on it. It used to creep up on me, like a silent snake with the most deadly bite. I didn't even understand them myself then. It took me a number of years before I was able to master them and not let them rule my life. I didn't want to take any pills for them. I had to start to learn to breathe.

During this time I was trying to accept myself the way I was, dealing with my own conflicting internal points of view. I was learning to love the part of me that society didn't like and didn't want me to be; I was learning to accept that I was different and that the way I saw the world was full of worthiness and love; I was on the road to learning and understanding that it can be acceptable to love more than one person at a time; and I was waiting to meet the people who would support me on my journey and love me just the way I was, multiple lovers and all.

Flowing

In Five Rhythms, "flowing" is the rhythm to connect with our inner truth; it is the art of following the flow of one's own organic energy. Flowing is listening to and attending to our deeper needs, while remaining receptive to both inner and outer stimuli. The corresponding element is Earth. It is about keeping oneself grounded and centred. When we are open to the flow of our physical selves, we can find doors leading to many wonderful pathways and we can begin to explore ourselves with extraordinary depth.

When I'm disconnected from the flow of my energy I am unable to perceive what is really happening inside and around me. When I am not present to my body I deny my own instincts and responses; I feel tired and am unable to move on to the next step in my life.

Dancing with flow has taught me to stop fighting who I am and to come to peace with myself in each and every moment. It has enabled me to let go of who I am not. Flowing never fails to help me just let things be, to let go of my need to control every situation.

I had just returned from my wonderful travel to the Greek islands and I felt immense excitement for the start of my new course: a year long intensive postgraduate study in the Physical Theatre principles of a famous French Artist called Lecoq. The course would comprise of mask-making, acrobatics, comedy, buffoonery, satire and storytelling with weekly self-created pieces, improvisation, movement, voice and circus skills. I was ready to dive in.

Life is full of synchronicity; the first person I met during the course was a lovely Greek man called **George**. Over the next year he would take me on journey of theatre, jazz, sensuality and anarchist modes of self-expression and allow me to find a new flow within.

My relationship with George was about flow and lack of flow in my life. He led me on a dance of letting go of what I knew before and seeing all the fresh delights and challenges that lay beyond. Although it was chaotic at times, the very essence of our relationship was flow. He taught me to eat slower, to lie in bed until noon, to sit still listening to jazz, to make a cigarette last for hours; and he acted as a gateway to help me start flowing with my sexual energy again, as my relationship with Hendrick had created deep insecurities about my abilities as a lover, girlfriend and woman.

October 2001

I feel alive; I arrive within myself to this creative path of physical theatre. The first person I meet as I enter the school steps is a Greek guy called George. I have to help him fill in his forms to register; his English is not very good. There are seven of us, all from different places in the world: South Africa, France, Spain, Spanish, Germany and a Danish girl. It is great to be creating and working on ourselves everyday from 9am – 6pm. It feels so right – great to hang out with people who all love art and theatre. This next year is for me; to be me in all the ways I wish to be.

20 November 2001

The course is going well; I am finding myself again. There is this character called George, the Greek guy I mentioned – he has this charming quality that moves me in every improvisation exercise he does. We have created a unique friendship. He cooks me dinners, I help him with his English, we sit in the Mark Rothko section of the Tate Modern, back to back, and talk within the silence that our bodies keep. It's wonderful.

I have decided that I will not live with Hendrick anymore and in the New Year I will move in with Amelie, the French girl and George. I feel very empowered by this decision. The three of us have created a great three-way friendship. They are older than me; we spend evenings drinking red wine, talking philosophy and about Grotowski (Polish theatre maker) and cooking dinners of new flavours.

This was an awfully big moment for me, given how important Hendrick was in my life. I realised that this next year wasn't just about a course; it was also about what I wanted and what I needed. I felt that living with Hendrick was holding me back from speaking the language of love, theatre and abstraction that I so desired. I also valued myself enough to know I needed a change; it wasn't healthy living and sharing the same bed with someone who was never going to touch me in the ways that I needed and deserved. Hendrick and I started to walk different paths.

30 November 2001

George's Greek ways lead me forth to the next moment in time. He gives me space to breathe, to play, to rediscover, to pretend. His love for jazz takes me on a new journey of notes into the worlds of Miles Davis and John Coltrane. I am a beginner in this new phase of philosophy and theatre of Lecoq; I am shy in the newness of rediscovering my sensual body.

I feel so horny all the time, the heat rushing through me every time he walks past. I am captivated. His passion allows me to let myself run wild; together we are creating a head-on collision.

28 January 2002.

All and nothing rages through me, as I feel myself giving and giving and giving and not getting back what I wish for. I love to love, that is my greatest passion, the passion of loving to love, loving to give; yet I am not doing it unconditionally? Deep down I yearn to be loved in return in the same passionate way.

New friends and the school overwhelm me, my little white lies cover up the real me and I feel safe behind the looking glass. Inside I am a jumbled mess of mixed tales, not knowing what is true and what is not.

I want to help people, care and love, share my wealth, help open people's minds to the truth, yet I need to find my truth first.

Here we see my passion for loving to love; I was disturbed that I was unable to meet people who would lay their hearts on their sleeves the way I would. It always appeared to me that people had conditional love notes attached to their backs and it was only when they would walk away that you could see what they wanted in return. After so much time being made a fool of, laughed at, judged and made to feel shameful, I too wanted to put a love note on my back, to ask to be loved the way I loved others; a defence against the pain. Yet this journey was all heading to one route: Love of oneself and acceptance of what is.

January 2002

The three of us have moved into an old council building in

East London, a bottom flat. It has a small garden and I have the outside room. Not sure what to make of this: Amelie and George have rooms that are back-to-back. I wonder what will happen with this dynamic. Will it work? The fourth member of the Stepney Green clan, a Serbian violinist; and so the four of us begin a new road together.

Hurt my ankle quite badly when I was back in South Africa. I have pulled all the ligaments again; it's the third time I have done this. Need to let it heal, which means I am not able to do a lot of the acrobatics. Why do I stop myself like this? Where do I not love myself enough?

This was a significant time in my life, as in the past I had hurt my ankles while taking drugs and not being aware. This final time, while back in South Africa, on a binge night really allowed me to step into that space of being the Saboteur. As soon as things were working in my life I would somehow find a way to injure my ankles. In turn it would allow me to stop myself reaching my fullest potential. I see this with my Acrobatics – I was unable to fully embark on this path as I had to rest and it took about six months to heal; even then it was not right.

3 February 2002

I love the three-way workings of my new friendship with Amelie and George. At times I feel jealousy when they spend time together; I need to trust in their love for me. We have something so beautiful.

I would love to call George a boyfriend, but he won't enter that story at all; I suppose I am one of his lovers and we continue to carry out our experiment with theatre, jazz, red wine and sex. I feel very fine with it. I am touched by his mad ways of conducting himself and his art.

My ability to flow with this three-way relationship led me to a much more open definition of love. It gave me wings to fly. I loved the three-way dynamic and all that it brought me. I never knew what the next moment would look like; all I could do was let each moment flow to the next. I was fascinated by the interplay of cultures between us, the different and amazing things we offered each other. We engaged on such a deep level of philosophy, theatre and just being who we needed to be in the moment.

2 August 2002

Since graduating, summer sings new tales. George continues to test me and I continue to let myself be tested. Our sexual explosions are happening more and more frequently. Summer is driving us dizzy with mojito-kissed hormones.

The other night George and I took the train to Brighton; we booked into room 508 along the beach front and watched the full moon, I bought champagne, he ordered moussaka, we chatted, made sweet love and he called me his Samanthula. I asked if we could be more, and he said he likes it when it's crunchy. So I spent the rest of the night crying outside on our 10 cm by 10 cm balcony while he just looked at me with eyes that gave me so much room to be full of all my bubbling emotions.

This strange open love has reached the point where I want more. This is all new for me, to flow with whatever is happening. I will let it be. His Greek ways teach me so much. I am also learning to put my little jealousy away, allow us to be what we are to each other and not expect anything more. It is really beautiful.

Brighton was one of those moments when I let myself be vulnerable and share with him that I wanted more. I knew he didn't want the burden of what words and language can do to a relationship, so he chose to keep it 'crunchy'. Underneath all the definitions, we had something beautiful and we both felt it. That was the main thing. I wasn't always able to see what it looked like or feel completely supported, but it just was what it was. I needed to learn how to flow with it, which is exactly what I did.

In the months leading to our departure for South Africa, George and I continued to go deep into the relationship we had created. Amelie and I started to work with a director and our newly devised Theatre Show.

That December I was bringing them both with me to South Africa for a six week travel. My last experience of bringing someone home wasn't so great, so deep down I was nervous, although I wasn't holding any expectations about what our three-way dynamic would look like in South Africa. I was just letting it all flow. December was an overload of events. The flow was beginning to gain momentum, and soon it would sweep me into the full swing of Staccato.

We took a long road-trip to the Kalahari Desert and this brought newness and change to our relationship. We were able to see each other's real selves and they were able to understand me more deeply through seeing how and where I had grown up. The trip had its little playful adventures: Amelie played French kiss with a friend of mine and George was strangely beginning to act like a boyfriend and my needs for affection, cuddles and warmth were being met.

After our road-trip to the desert we experienced a terrifying hijacking nightmare on Christmas Eve which left me shaken up. Amelie and I were getting a lift home when all of a sudden three well-dressed Asian youngsters jumped out of the nearby car and one of them asked, "Miss, do you have directions...". He hadn't even finished his sentence when two guns came out, one to my head and the other to Amelie's. I gave him my bag with money, cards and all inside.

"Puton, merde jet la fuck off," Amelie screamed. I turned to see her fighting the man who was trying to take her bag. One of the guys was screaming in half-baked English Afrikaans slang "shhhooooootttt heeeerrrr, shoooooootttt her." She threw her beer in the man's face; they finally got her bag

97

and left without a bullet being fired. The incident shook me to the core. I couldn't believe this was happening in South Africa. I knew it had become more dangerous, but not this much. Hearing people's responses – including my dad's – was even more frightening. They responded as if this was an everyday thing for them; they were casual, laid back and just glad I hadn't been hurt.

The attack damaged my ability to trust and to feel safe. Still to this day, if a situation frightens me, my body can go into panic mode and I become full of fear, like I am being transported back to that December in 2003.

These days, South Africa is not a safe place by any means; I am not sure what has caused this crime wave. The different class systems? The "have's" and "have not's"? The gangs in the squatter camps? The illegal immigrants from surrounding African countries? Zimbabwe? The corrupt police system? No electricity? I feel it is all of these things. It will take a while before South Africa is able to stand strong, but I believe in the people and it can be done. It is such a vibrant land with a sacred heart and true freedom brewing on the horizon.

I felt like I was the character in *Run Lola Run* with a time bomb waiting to go off. South Africa was not safe to be in; George was sweet and affectionate with me, but I felt like I wanted something else, the feeling of rage brewing again as soon as we started to get intimate. My anxiety had started to come back and I decided to stop working on my theatre show with Amelie; my heart wasn't in it. My heart and soul were off somewhere else; I wasn't sure where. I wasn't sure what I wanted to do.

A new year was waiting for me and I needed to digest, wind down, detox, sleep and just be myself for a while. So many thoughts and new ideas were running through my head. All I wanted to do was run, but run where? Who would take me? Where could I go that was far enough away? Who would handle my chorus-line of never-ending thoughts and emotions? The flowing had led me to take a sharp and definite move into my Staccato. I decided to run away from everything familiar; I went to Australia.

When I arrived back in London I took all the money I had, phoned my aunt in Australia and within a week I was flying high through time-zones, over oceans and islands, getting further away from everything and everyone I knew. My visa was for six months, but if I wanted I could extend it. I was thrilled. It felt so sudden, so final; I was leaving London for an indeterminate time. I was following the final part of my wave and I was about to dance a whole new rhythm.

Everything was falling into place. I trusted my instinct more than I ever had before; all the little voices of self-destructive babbling were switched off.

I believe that the only constant thing in life is change. All of us reach the point where we need a change in perspective and there is something about being removed from familiar contexts that helps us achieve insightful clarity. Here I was finding a new angle on my life and figuring out a new plan. The past year had been a whirlwind of events, triangles, theatre, red wine, accents, deadlines and jazzy mornings with George. I flowed with it all and then I reached a point where I needed to assert myself, to find out what I wanted to say "yes" to and what I wanted to say "no" to.

I had learned to flow through all the discomfort in my relationship with George and now I saw that the relationship wasn't what I wanted anymore. What was I looking for? I just knew it wasn't what I had been living.

Staccato

Staccato in The Five Rhythms is the gateway to the heart; it is the rhythm of our relationship with everyone, including ourselves. It shows us how to step into the world outside, how to connect with our feet, hearts and feelings. This rhythm is the leader of the warrior within us. Its movements are defined by sharp edges and finished extensions. Its element is fire. It is about connecting to our fiery sexual centre, where kundalini energy and creativity reside. It is the part of us that stands up for who we are, who we love, what we love, what we are passionate about. Staccato is the fierce teacher of boundaries. It's about saying yes and no and making clear decisions and seeing them through.

Dancing Staccato grounds my emotions, decisions and energies. It is a great tool for when I encounter emotional turmoil in my life. It calls me to be disciplined, to be a clear communicator and to connect with my creativity and sexuality. It is a powerful guide to understanding how I extend from my heart centre into the world with courage and truth.

This next period in my life was a ride through various events that can best be expressed by the Staccato beat. I was beginning to relate to everyone around me through my heart centre; I was practising saying "yes" and "no" and I was discovering the vast importance of clear boundaries. Communication with myself and others became clearer. I was working out what I wanted from the next phase of my life.

My main relationship during this time was with Tony; he arrived some time after my trip to Australia. In the meantime I flew far across the ocean to find a new me. A grounded me? An artistic me? An adventurous me? I didn't have a plan, I didn't want a plan – I wanted to take one day at a time, follow the signs, do lots of reading, write, splash in the ocean, run for miles, eat healthily, travel to places I didn't know and meet new people everywhere. I was looking for connections with those around me and I was ready to explore whatever those connections might be.

24 January 2003

Staying in the hills of north Sydney; it's beautiful. Went for a run and caught up on my sleep. Feeling quite surreal this morning. I am far away from all I know.

"There is a presence that is larger than me, that has been with me all my life."

Started reading a book called "In the Meantime" about love being the levels of a house: starting in the basement and making our way up to create a relationship that lives in the attic of love at the top of the house. It's fascinating.

Realising that George fuels me creatively and sexually. I have regained my confidence but emotionally and spiritually I wish to leave, he is not the one for me. I am not moving forward spiritually with him. I need to not need him or want him anymore.

February 2003

My days here have been beautiful, quiet, full of running, fresh air, space to think, time to start writing my book. What am I so afraid of about my writing? I always start at the beginning and then leave it at that; I need to face the middle and the end. Many mornings I kayak to Shark Island in Rose Bay. Sip coffee outside the Sydney bridge, spend money I am not making, read as much I can about this process called SELF-DEVELOPMENT.

Last night I lay naked with my aunt in the splashing of the midnight waves, with tiny phosphorescence dancing all over our bodies like wild magic fire. We thought it was God; later today we were told it was baby jellyfish hatching from their eggs. It was the most extraordinary experience I have had all year.

"Love is not about the other person, it's all about you in your isolation and then moving it into reality; then people and beautiful gifts begin to appear."

Being back in nature helped me to process all that had happened. It gave me the space and distance to start seeing how I had created everything in my life so far, and how I could start taking more responsibility for my actions. It gave me space from my London world and from the mad and sad tales that I was still digesting after having my freedom taken away by the whole hijacking incident.

Australia gave me a safety net I wasn't used to. I could sleep with the doors open at night and taste a new freedom of space. Within my very being I was opening up to the strong sexual energy that has always been with me. A new part of my sexual core was being activated.

I wanted to play with this new buzzing energy inside, and play with it I did. I began not to care what people thought and just like Staccato I hopped from one moment to the next, from one man to the next, from one tale to the next; from one rock pool to another; from mistake to mistake. It was liberating. I travelled to Melbourne and finally ended up in Adelaide which saw my promiscuous side come out in full force. For the first few weeks I made out with a different guy every night.

Whether it was the summer heat or being so far away from everything I knew, I was in the full rush of my summer hormones and playfulness. An English solo traveller named James was sweet and shy – we stripped down in the harbour and went skinny-dipping and made out alongside the sea-lions. Then, to slow the pace down, I found a lovely fit for the rest of my stay – a very sexy surfer, traveller and healer named Nick. I found myself making love to him so sweetly.

Aside from all the boys, the dates and the travelling, I got to spend a great deal of time with myself, soul searching. I read and explored numerology, metaphysical healing and many other esoteric practices. My Aunt, who is a healer, shared with me all her modalities from books, oils, herbs, lymphatic drainage and reiki.

I soon made my way back to Sydney, I knew I needed to get back to London, to pick up where things had been left off. I was ready to face George and my reality I had left behind. I was ready to move out of the house, to find a job in the West End and to start trusting myself and my choices.

A part of me came to life in Australia; my heart allowed herself to be filled with many new loves and attractions. I seemed to be able to beat freely there. I didn't care what other people thought; I found a space to be free, to kiss freely, to make mistakes, to create connections even if I didn't know where they were going. I danced in the summer sun and gave love to all around me and most important I gave love to myself.

Australia opened me up to a deeper part of myself. I saw that although I enjoyed my playful side and the great experiences it offered me, I didn't need to rely on it for validation. A part of me also needed to be wanted by others; having a lover close to me gave me the validation and intimacy I was looking for.

I knew the importance of touch and intimacy; I wanted it from all my friendships. I saw it as a given part of any relationship, although I wasn't always sure how to initiate it. I let myself be guided by my instincts and my new toolbox: responsibility, effort, love, honesty and surrender.

When I arrived back in London, I needed to end things with George and make it final. This was very tricky as we were still living in the same space – so I needed to find a new place.

George and I ended our creative romantic endeavour with one last night of good old-fashioned hotel frolicking. We drank beer all afternoon then we found a cosy hotel near Russell Square. We ripped up the sheets and played like monkeys on Ecstasy, then fell into a deep slumber, waking in the evening for a late Indian dinner, red wine and great stimulating conversation.

We went to sleep cuddled like true childhood sweethearts and when the morning sun streamed in I didn't feel I had the strength to leave. But then we walked to the tube station, we kissed one last time; he took the northbound and I headed south to my new transit destination, in Clapham Common.

What was I looking for? It all seemed to be linked with sex; somewhere deep within, my intuition was trying to show me something. I had always found sexual play (in all forms, whether it was a hug, a kiss, an embrace, or a blowjob) to be a form of healing; it was a way to let go of something inside, a way to get love, a way to show people who I was, to show people I loved them and above all, it was the way I most fully expressed myself.

It isn't only sex that intrigued me, it was also a whole world of cuddling and being extremely tactile that made so much sense to me. I wanted to share it with everyone who crossed my path. What did it all mean? What was my intuition pointing at? I had so many questions firing through my mind that it often felt overwhelming.

I was looking for something new, a place where I could create my own truth, where I was free to love people and be loved in return, a space where there was no distinct right or wrong; a space to be naked, a space to dance with my many partners, a space to take risks and be supported all the way. A space to play around sexually, a space to be open, a space to cry, to be artistic, a space to be a part of a community, a space to breathe, to communicate, to not be judged. A space to really find myself and above all, a space to be honest.

That summer in London unfolded with captivating charm; I worked on the West End, made friends with my Spanish workmates, flirted with women, read scripts, worked on surreal shows and live performances, moved into a great new house with a loud bunch of Italian lesbians, smoked joints in the alleyway of the Piccadilly theatre, toured to Austria to take part in a festival. There were late-night writing sessions, late-night beer drinking sagas, late-night dancing sessions and many late-night flings that all seemed to overlap and tell me a story.

Sometime late in August I auditioned for a role in Madame Tussaud's Chamber of Horrors. It was a gruelling ordeal, but one week later I got my first paid acting job. I'm not sure if running around with blood dripping from your lips in dark dungeons and scaring people makes one a successful actress, but it was fulfilling enough, making people rush in all directions to find the exit because I'd scared them.

This all took place deep down below the tarmac on Baker Street. We had our own rules, our own lighting, our own dress code, our own timetable and our very own set in the strobe-lit madness that became my home.

It was my first real experience working with British people – their coldness, their cynical humour, their agelessness, their accents that differ from region to region, their love of fry-ups, plus their intellectual banter and everyday drinking down at the local pub. I soon found myself a regular at the Globe. Many pints later I was forming fantasies of every guy who worked with me. I subtly played the game of releasing my South African charms, seducing and being seduced back in the cages of surreal day-to-day screams, of high and low pitches and mixed accents, of swearing slang. The naughty play in the dark was fuelling a side of me that needed to come out.

Late autumn brought doom, gloom and Christmas 'cheers'. I

found myself at the pub again, flirting my way through beer, when Tony – one of my work mates – asked me to come home with him.

Tony was different: weird, mysterious, his gestures revealing a resemblance to David Blaine. He took me to bed and we made sweet English love. We poured out our rejected and hurting hearts to each other and began a secret romance, deep within our safe-haven of makeup, fake blood, Jack-the-Ripper street costumes and dark alleyways.

Secrets never stay secrets for long and we soon fell easily into the role of boyfriend and girlfriend; it worked for a while. I met his parents, we spent time in movies, plotted horror scripts, travelled through the mind of David Blaine, talked at length about ghosts (Tony was able to see them quite clearly). We meandered through pub nights of drunken chatter, drunken kisses, drunken erections and drunken moments laced with a foggy love.

My not wanting to be touched (except on my own terms) took Tony through a dizzy ping-pong game of yes and no. I continued to lead him on through the New Year with mixed signals: every time I called it off he came back to me and we would start all over again. We would have a few days of passion and then I would smash it, like a vase broken into many pieces; he always cleaned up after me. I didn't know how to say thank you. I just kept trying to seek the truth.

What was this truth that I kept searching for? Every time we were intimate I would feel the rage build in me and I needed to sabotage what we were creating. This was done by cheating and being with other people behind his back. It allowed me to feel that I was still attracted to other people and that there was nothing wrong with me. It allowed me to numb the rage and anger brewing inside.

January 2004

I am feeling these horrible sensations when we make love. It feels so confusing. Is this what it feels like for all people when they are in relationships. Something huge is waking me up and I don't know how to access it or how to read and understand my feelings around this.

I feel very distant from that part of myself that knows how to be fully present; I get lost in this world of drunken, drug-fuelled evenings. I am just letting it all be, trying not to be too hard on myself. I need to start being honest with those around me, with those I play with, those I love. Trying to be honest and finding it so difficult to tell Tony how I feel.

My honesty would develop in stages: I still wasn't honest with myself, so I couldn't be honest with those around me. I wasn't honest with Tony about why I didn't like his touch; I made out that it was him, not me. This defence mechanism protected me from looking into what was really going on.

I was also slowly realising that I didn't want to be connected in ways that were always based around alcohol, drugs and late nights; I wanted something else. So I kept going back and forth like a yo-yo – it was pure staccato: one moment I wanted to get drunk, smoke, be wild, let the madness flow and have sex; the next moment I wanted to be still, meditate, read books, run and eat healthy. It was a constant jump from yes to no and no to yes, and I let it all ride itself all the way through. It was also at this time I met an American who would bring a powerful element of Truth and Honesty into my life.

February 2004

Freedom Community

I have joined this amazing community of people who are largely based in the States. It's called Freedom Community. The conversations have blown me out the water. Such clarity, honesty and openness with each other; I am not sure what to expect or what will come of this. I feel intimidated and out of my depth.

March 2004

I talk bullshit, I talk truth. I feel one way one moment and the next moment it completely changes and I am left with the contradiction. Why am I always on the search for the experience of a guy who will heal me and love me and be with me? Who will love me, no matter what? Who will give me freedom? I am looking for someone who will not mind if I kiss someone else and allow my wild horse to gallop off.

Impulsive? I feel I am taking Tony for a long ride through my emotional rollercoaster of fears and findings. I don't love him; I love that he loves me so much, that he keeps running back after all my cheating. I love the idea of having a boyfriend. The sex thing is once again getting very hard to deal with; one moment I want him, the next moment I want to bite him, to puncture his skin with anger. Where are these feeling coming from? Sex with people on a casual basis seems fine, yet in relationships, anger and hurt haunt me. I'm scared and I don't know what to do about it.

It felt like I was riding a dizzy rollercoaster. My relationship with Tony was stuck in the shadow side of Staccato: with him I would feel like a "maybe", so I would say "yes", and then immediately after, say "no". I knew it was gaining momentum for something more chaotic to happen. I was being as honest as I could, but it is very hard when you are stuck deep in confusion. Everything I said and felt became one giant contradiction.

Months at the Chamber slipped by; the highs and lows of my rollercoaster through destruction and self-discovery were about to hurtle me through new and crazy ways of finding myself. The following months saw my truths, freedoms, sexuality and contradictions play out to the fullest. It was as though I were watching myself from above or on a movie screen.

I started a new job backstage at the Lyric, a famous theatre in the West End, on a musical called *The Beautiful and the Damned*. It is the love story of Zelda and Scott Fitzgerald and their destructive relationship around cocaine and the affluent and hedonistic lifestyle of the 1920s. The show seemed to run parallel to my own life.

One night, after too much booze and pub crawling, I ended up in my first threesome with two friends. The bath water kept pouring over the edges, more Ecstasy in my blood stream, more orgasms spreading themselves on the sheets of my double bed. The heat and passion of being with an English, well-built lad and a Brazilian sex goddess played out in a three week triangle. Daniel cooked two breakfasts each morning, ran two baths, gave two orgasms and had two ladies in his arms each night as we three drifted into drunken sleep. We three dated each other certain it would work out, but drugs, lack of sleep and crazy three-way dynamics got the better of us. I walked away with my first threesome under my belt.

March 2004

Woke up this morning to my sweet threesome, headed to Tony to try to break it off properly, but ended up in bed with him and denying anything was wrong. Why can't I just be honest?

My honesty about my sexual play with others would come in stages. I knew I was withholding the truth from my other lovers; I didn't give them a chance, because I didn't want to be judged or to have to explain myself to anyone. Tony knew I was seeing other people, yet I did not tell him all the truth and made him feel like he was still the most important thing.

Was I selective with the truth to make myself feel safe? To protect myself? To allow myself some privacy? To not take full responsibility? To not come across as a complete nymphomaniac? To not come across as the bad girl? Looking back, it was all these reasons and more. It took me a few more years to start to link it all together and find my place in this world of relationships, connections, sexual liberation and healing.

22 March 2004

I tease you, I pull you along on my destructive search for happiness, like some science experiment. Today I told Tony about my threesome. It broke his heart. It was the last straw. I need to give him time, to give myself time. I feel so hungry for all these experiences, like some wild animal has opened a door inside me; I am scared about where it is going to lead. It did feel good to be honest and not have to lie about what happened – a new step on my quest for honesty and truth.

The people I meet through this Freedom Community website in the States continue to inspire me into a new way of being. I haven't met them at all. There's a wedding in Paris where I can meet some of them – so I've bought a ticket to go and hang out with total strangers! I feel like I am vibrating on some crazy strange level of wanting everything. Sucking, searching and squeezing the juice from every resource. I just want to spread this love I have inside my chest with everyone. Some people it works with, others it becomes a messy saga.

My feeling of not wanting to be touched is gathering speed; the idea of committing to a relationship brings up a deep anger within me. I am not sure where these feelings came from. Did something happen to me? Was I abused? Don't be silly Sam, it's something that will go away, just be patient.

The Staccato rhythm showed up clearly in regard to truth and communication. I was only just beginning to skim the outlines of what may or may not have happened to me when I was younger. I was still only selectively honest. I wanted to feel I had control in every situation and if I did tell people the real truth, I would lose that control. I just wasn't ready for that space of deep vulnerability.

I needed to ride my rollercoaster over the edge and see what would happen. So that is what I did. My next relationship would be the most chaotic relationship I had experienced, in every way possible, and even though I knew what might lie ahead, I threw myself in. I thought I might be able to put on the brakes if things became too much, but as it turned out, the brakes had been removed.

Chaos

In the context of five rhythms, Chaos allows us to break free from our illusions as it hurtles us headlong into the beat. It takes us on a journey from "I can't" to "I will". The practice of Chaos immediately brings us back to our bodies in the present moment. This rhythm liberates us from restrictive ideas about who we are and gives us a real experience of being free, intuitive and creative. The corresponding element is water, which is always changing speed, momentum and shape.

The shadow side of chaos is that it can throw us into the psychic panic of being overwhelmed. In my voyage with **Gavin** I tapped into the dark and destructive side of Chaos. I found myself ungrounded. Chaos led me through a dizzy dance of being flooded with unfinished moments and I often felt isolated, alone and tired.

Understanding the importance of Chaos has enabled me to

explore the unknown. Chaos is the practice of delving into that unknown, not fearing what one might find on the other side, and riding the creative wave. This rhythm has carried me through family disputes, break-ups and the fear of my own success. It has been a great mentor, teaching me how to move through all the chaos of life and to find, deep within the mayhem, the serenity of grace.

For me, Chaos and Gavin go hand-in-hand. The whirlwind of our relationship started on ungrounded turf. I knew things were gaining momentum in my life and I thought my firmer roots would enable me to handle the storm. I wasn't prepared for all that Gavin brought along with him. I went against everything I believed in. I stayed with him in the hope that I might change him, make him a happier person, heal and fix his wild complexities. I couldn't have been more wrong.

My friendships that I had started making with the Freedom Community were growing, so I decided to go to Paris to meet some of these people and to find out more about this website that I had joined so unreservedly. Freedom Community sees people from all walks of life, including artists, lawyers, bankers, chefs, flight attendants, bar tenders, workshop leaders, college professors, performers and more. It is a place for experiencing and celebrating our diversity, our passions, our challenges and our greatest joys. It started from a strong friendship between two friends: one wanted to bring community into his everyday play, while the other's goal was to bring freedom into people's lives. They posed the question, "What would it take for you to be free?" So the name Freedom Community spread and our tribe started. These people have been an integral part of my life, helping me become the person I am today.

The main principles of Freedom Community are tools for experiencing our own and others' fullest self-expression and authentic communication. They rest upon the core pillars of honesty, integrity and choice.

The conversations were unlike any other I had experienced: filled with deep inquiry, radical honesty and sincere love. This community also celebrates open sexuality and this was a draw card for me from the beginning. The way open relationships were navigated within the community was clear, a drama-free, safe and honest space. Sharing with each other about safe sex practices was crucial and there was full acknowledgement of one another's highest truth.

Freedom Community has given me friendships, life experiences, sexual exploration, travels, truths and insights into who I am. Above all else, it has shown me what is possible with friendship when we walk the path of being a stand for each other and our freedom.

April 2004

I find myself in Paris meeting these amazing people from America. We've never met before, but when we introduced ourselves at the hotel I felt like I have known them all my life.

Four days of no drinking, coffee-fuelled walks through old cobbled streets, endless midnight conversations and a new way of hanging out with people – this gives me tingles.

One of the friends I am sharing a room with asked if we could cuddle. No one has ever asked to cuddle me. We slept like spoons all night. It was so yummy. Nothing attached, nothing happened, it was wonderful and healing. I felt really honoured.

This trip was very important. I loved the fact that I was able to spend the night with a friend and have nothing happen;

yet still have all my needs met because I was wrapped up in his arms. It showed me that there were people who were up for playing this game that I didn't quite have the words for then; it was about connecting with those around me without it always leading to sexual play. This was very refreshing.

Late April 2004

Back in London. Paris fuels me with possibilities. I wish to create with my friends here like I did in Paris. I have been hearing about this course called Landmark Education. Most people in the Freedom Community have done it. I am going to look into it. I feel it could push me through to the next part of my game. The game of honesty.

The Landmark Forum is a powerful experience; it continues to have a major impact on how I live my life. So what exactly is Landmark Education? For me, it was a three-day course that assembled 150 people from all walks of life into a small loft suite in the heart of central London. The course examined our blind spots and asked us to take a look at areas of our lives where we felt we lacked power, closure, happiness and success. The course examines how you can live your life powerfully when you are honest with yourself and others. It's not about achieving happiness at some point in the future; it is about being happy and honest in the present moment and inspiring those around you into the same mode of being. It helps you to separate your past from your future and to live with the certainty that anything is possible.

My Forum experience was extremely powerful, and it has been one of the most important catalysts in my life. It paved the way for me to see my own lies and dishonesty and to start communicating in a powerful way; I learned to address my past lies in a way that set me free and respected others. I phoned my dad and shared with him my feelings about stealing the money and why I had done it; I was able to forgive myself and start a new fresh relationship with my dad based on the possibility of being truly honest. I phoned my past boyfriends and told them about my lies and cheating. Some just laughed and others thanked me. Others I still haven't been able to get hold of and so I have left those to the cosmos to resolve.

It was amazing to just come clean with things. I felt the lightest I had in years. Landmark gave me the insight I needed to address my issues with open communication and honesty.

After playing with how to integrate this new work into my current life, and how to figure out the next steps in my creative path, my world pressed pause as Gavin caught me off guard while I was on a summer drinking binge. From the moment we met, everything began to slowly spin out of control. I thought that the tools I had from the course would help me stay afloat, but at the time they didn't. I took a massive step back in order to take a huge leap forward.

I had been drinking all evening and at 3am I invited everyone at the pub back to my house for a little after-drinks house party. Working in the West End opened up a whole underground world of late-night drinking, private bars and lines of white powder. Once we arrived at my place I rushed up the stairs and grabbed two Ecstasy pills from my flatmates; they had a large glass bottle full of different-coloured pills for all occasions.

Not knowing Gavin from a bar of soap, I put a pill in his mouth and jumped on to my wild horse. Our connection was established. The rest of the morning was a big adventure. Sunrise had us roaming Finsbury Park with make-believe javelins, laughing ourselves into silly stupors and hugging trees. We made our way to Soho's outdoor swimming oasis where we acted like madly-crazed children, splashing away in total love of each magical moment. Nothing sexual happened between us and I was sure it would stay that way.

This paved the way for a very passionate, stormy, unstable and dangerous love affair. I was hooked from the moment we began. It seemed that for the first time someone was wilder and wackier than I was. How would I keep up? How could I get him to be still? And how was I to ever find the strength to let him go?

Gavin was Gavin. No words can capture his highs and lows, his love for life and his deep sadness; his contradictions were what made him special.

I threw myself into things so deeply that I couldn't have stopped if I'd wanted to. And I didn't want to; his charming spell worked its way through my neurons and I lost myself deeply within his world. Every day was another riddle, another pint, another bar to close, another Beatles song, another park to explore, another day to lose and find your keys, another day to read the Sun, another mash and gravy, another day to reconstruct myself.

I somehow forgot I could leave the relationship if I chose to and I reached the lowest point of my own self-destruction. My lust and passion to change him, mixed with my mothering instincts to fix, overrode my higher intentions for myself.

The best aspects of Gavin were his spontaneity, his sensitivity and his ability to make people laugh. He taught me about being vulnerable and really living on the edge. His drinking combined with his complex psychology made a potent mixture. His highs were very high, I would sail away on cloud nine; and then just like that I wouldn't be able to track him down for days. I would have to wait and wait until the lows had passed.

July 2004

The summer is filled with new people in my life: new loves, new experiences and new music. Gavin fills my head with old Beatles melodies and his voice is so beautiful. His lush Liverpudlian accent has me hanging on each vowel. I am so infatuated with the idea of this man who is also yet such a boy.

I have started working on a new show that I will be taking to Austria for Halloween. Working with a Palestinian/Canadian woman called Isha. Her strong background and crazy characters bring light and endless passion for creation. I am excited to see where this creative theatrical venture will lead us.

I started out with my intentions in the right place. Gavin was someone I liked, but I was aware our lifestyles were very different. I was going to keep it cool and casual. Soon, that reserve washed away and my love and lust for him took me into deep needing, wanting and dark desire. Our relationship was fuelled by night-time pub-crawling, cocaine and Ecstasy extravaganzas (this saw us both indulge in wild orgies, threesomes and naked shenanigans).

His moods didn't ring any bell of alarm for me and I kept pressing on; I thought that he would soon come around to my world. His charming, endless energy hid his difficulties and most of the time I took his word that he had this handled. Then I began tumbling headfirst into chaos. I started to lose sight of what was important to me: my health, my work, my mental stability, my spirituality and my friends; my community and my honesty to self and others.

He had his own agenda, his own timing, his own clock and his own game plan. After two months of his magic spell, he moved in with me on his own terms. He would arrive most nights at 5am, knocking on my door, singing me songs and sleeping his hangover away until mid-morning. I often missed work. At times I would just watch him sleep – it was when he was the most peaceful.

Most nights he would sleepwalk, he would crash about my room and bump into things. I developed a real need to mother him, to take care of him and to try to show him another way. His Orange voicemail service was all I got from him most of the time.

Slowly, I found myself living though his rollercoaster states. There was something very wrong and his charming disguise was wearing away.

My life of chasing after someone who was not there came crashing down when I got a phone call from Gavin, late one November night, in a terrible state. What should I do? How was I to handle myself in this situation? I wanted to help him, but my healing juices were running dry.

Gavin had this very strange way of showing how he felt emotionally; just before the winter broke I received a text message from him that said, "Parker will be very cold without his Penelope around". I was off to South Africa to rest, rebuild and rejuvenate. Deep under all his hurts and confusion he deeply cared about me, but he could only communicate this through a reference to *Thunderbirds*; I was his Penelope and he was my Parker.

I left for South Africa that Christmas. Where had I been for the last six months? I was waking up from a sleepy, surreal dream. I felt slow; I needed rest. My body was at zero-energy and my heart was very fragile. It felt like I had been dancing for months with no water and no break. I couldn't fix him. It wasn't my job to fix him; he needed to want to help himself. So I flew off into the sun and tried to regain my sense of perspective.

14 February 2005

I am slowly digesting Gavin and releasing all the old energies of attachment. I am feeling lighter. I'm understanding that everything has a purpose; things are simple if you let them be. I am becoming more honest about what I want. Getting this new job with Kevin Spacey at The Old Vic provides me with new faces, new attractions, new meetings, new thespians and new creative goals. It's really amazing working among all these celebrities who walk in and out of the building.

I have moved in with my Palestinian Friend Isha and we have this crazy house where people come and go, shag, scream, eat and fight, laugh, cry, party, sleep, do drugs, do yoga, meditate, write plays, watch films, paint, and express themselves. It is a house that provides me with wisdom to learn tolerance.

Isha and I are working on a two-woman show about cultural differences. We will be putting it on at the Old Vic Theatre and taking it to Jordan in the summer.

I am in daily conversation with my friends from the States and each month a new beautiful being is met and I take him or her around London as though we were old-time friends. The connections feel real and honest. I love having this Freedom Community in my life.

I am single for the first time and it feels so refreshing. I feel like things are starting to manifest all around me, it's really special to see how nothing happens for nothing – that everything is interlinked.

What is manifestation work? I believe that our spiritual body is composed of fields of energetic vibration. When we are in right alignment with this blueprint, so to speak, it works like the Law of Attraction: What you put out there you will create, and this creation is best described as manifestation. It's knowing that we are the masters of our own lives and we can create anything we wish for. If we follow the signs, become clear in our intentions for what we want, then we can start to witness the thread of events that show up in our lives and bring us to the right place at the right time.

With all these new manifestations showing up around me I decided to hold my first FREEDOM EVENT. A Freedom Event is a magical space: a party with a totally different design. It is an organised event that usually runs for twelve hours and starts with a welcome circle where the group gets to meet each other, to learn the rules of the game for the night and to discuss what the next twelve hours will look like.

Each event is different. In the past I have seen some really creative worlds manifest. The rules of the game stay the same: open and honest communication at all times, no closed doors, total responsibility for your communication – no matter what you have had to drink or ingest. In my experience, although alcohol and drugs can be available at events, they are always used with consciousness and self-awareness.

My first event was called *The Rhythm of Love* and was about connecting to our inner child and allowing ourselves space to be kids again in a safe and structured environment.

2 March 2005

Rhythm of Love Event

Held my first Freedom Community gathering, at my home. The event was called "The Rhythm of Love". Ten people from the States flew over for it. The idea was to create an intentional party where people could come together as friends in an open environment to express themselves at all levels without being judged. It was about getting in touch with our inner child, so I had body painting set up, there was dancing, we got to draw, play drums, paint, sing and just be like children again. The space we kept was truly magical and I am so thrilled to be a part of this community. Not sure where it will lead as it seems that I am only able to connect with these beautiful people about twice a year. When I do I am the most whole and complete ever. Just interesting to observe for the meantime.

The event I held in London allowed me to let go of the last traces of hurt I had been holding onto about Gavin. It grounded me into trusting that everything happens for a reason, and that I was fully responsible for all the choices I had made in the past and would make in the future. Despite the shadow and craziness of the chaos that had swept me away, I was grateful for finding my tools for honesty and for discovering a community in which I could be loved and celebrated: Landmark Forum and Freedom Community, two beautiful creations that anchored my chaos and helped me see the magical threads of connection, interaction and possibility.

I felt I was stepping into an enchanted new world where

people communicate, share and support each others' possibilities, where they laugh, travel and have open relationships. And all of this was built on honesty, something I had so deeply struggled with in the past.

AN OPEN RELATIONSHIP

Lyrical

The Lyrical rhythm shows us how to break out of destructive patterns and to surrender into the depths of our fluid, creative, soulful selves – it is a guide to discovering the integrity and dignity that we often forget is within us. Lyrical is an expression in all its forms and shapes; it connects us to humanity, timelessness, patterns, cycles; it teaches us how to be light. The element that navigates Lyrical is air – flowing and magical. Lyrical is about playing, exploring new routes, connecting with our inner child and dancing to the rhythm of love.

If we didn't experience Lyrical, we would never let things mature in our lives. We get caught too easily in the destructive echoes of self-doubt, physical addictions and overwork. We go through the motions and we stop questioning our habits and rituals. We fall asleep at the wheel and we stop being able to see the true miracles all around us.

I feel my own life has always had a lyrical aspect, although it hasn't been constant. When I make it through the porthole into my lyrical moments, moments of being, of dancing, I open up to what I really love; the power in the obstacles around me diminish. This is the rhythm that dissolves all that no longer serves us and plugs us into the sacredness of everyday life. Lyrical teaches us how to play and be light.

Chaos made its way out through the back door and Lyrical energy moved through me. I was blessed and grateful for the beautiful form in which it arrived: **Jacques**. Jacques' French accent echoed through me the moment we met. I believe my first words to him were, "Are you gay?" This started a warm dialogue between the two of us. I found myself instantly loving this foreign, curly-head boy.

He was from another time and era – a young French-Canadian bohemian poet, reading the beat novels of Jack Kerouac, Rimbaud, Verlaine and Henry Miller. He brought me back to life with his endless letters and his love for Edith Piaf. His guitar tunes opened my heart and I fell in love so truly, so, so innocently – just like I was sixteen all over again. This was a wonderfully authentic and playful chapter in my life

13 March 2005

After the beers began to talk I took this French guy home with me and he ended up in my bed. We made such beautiful love; he was so present to my body, touching me as though I hadn't been touched before, his kisses perfectly fitted with mine. I believe kisses are so important, they reveal so much about someone. He has innocence about him – though through his travels and hitchhiking across the States and South America he has acquired a unique independence. I have no expectations as to where this may lead; I just know that it felt so comfortable this morning as we kissed each other good-bye. There was something else leading us, some invisible love elves singing sweetly overhead.

20 May 2005

My heart is alive, blood thumping through the vessels, breathing life into new spaces. I woke up in a desert unable to breathe and my thirst parched. I found a bottle of you and I poured you down. You are most refreshing water; my organs are cleansed, my heart renewed, my feet recharged to walk again into another love tale. Another epic love story with me as the star.

You taste so cold and so hot. You are both sweet and sour. So full of all the elements. Fiery passion, driven by music, poetry and literature. Watery with all your emotions, female and male alike. Airy as you follow your heart and walk the clouds of your dreams, your imaginings of love fill my view. Earthy as you care and recycle my ways, ways that hold me back. You connect to the reality of the human condition, to the beggar on the street, to the banker who drinks his double malt. You are way beyond your years.

I am falling, slipping, sliding, running and melting in love with you.

29 May 2005

Jacques is very blunt with his speaking and it often puts him at the centre of extended laughter at work. I let my heart run wild with him; I pour my love sagas and past out onto him. He always has a way to relate them back to a novel he has read, so I can find peace of mind. His very French-ness makes him so romantic by nature. I am thrilled. I am dazzled. I don't feel triggered by his touch.

The two-woman show Isha and I are writing is making way

and it's the most exciting thing I have done creatively. I love it. To write and create one's own work is something so remarkably rewarding.

The show was called *The Journey to Hell*. It was about two characters who embark on a journey around the world, one a white South African Christian, the other a coloured Palestinian Muslim. Their journey together enables them to explore tolerance, understanding and compassion. The style we used was dark satire and we played more than fifteen different characters each. It was a great achievement. We wrote it, performed it, directed it and produced it, and we got to have a few days at the Old Vic Theatre.

Opening nights are always a big deal, I was very nervous. I downed at least half a bottle of rescue remedy and just let the rest flow. To take charge of one's own creativity is a wonderful feeling; to make people laugh is a huge achievement and to inspire people to be more tolerant, to challenge them to become more loving - that feels transformational.

2 June 2005

Tonight my show opens; to say I am scared is an understatement – though having seen Neil Diamond perform amongst thousands of fans last night gives me renewed hope and confidence.

Things with Jacques and I are slow; it's right for me, it's right for him. We care, we play and we laugh all the time.

Isha and I have become deeply close since working together; we do everything with each other. It's a little like a marriage contract (except with no sex). She makes me see things with new eyes. Her stories land with me very strongly – she has endured many horrid hardships of hatred when visiting her homeland, Palestine, a country Israel still does not recognise, a country that is fought for daily with weapons and bloodshed; her people try to gain a piece of the freedom, a piece of land that they can call home.

I am opening up to the world of Islam and what's really behind it. It's fascinating to hear her stories and notice our differences.

Friendship is a beautiful thing, and the differences between people can create contrasts, make the friendship full of flavour and deep learnings. Isha and I have always been different – we come from opposite ends of the globe – but our passion for art, theatre and comedy, silly play, late-night tales and love for travel connected us immediately.

Our journey together mirrored our show and when I went with Isha to Jordan that summer I was confronted with another part of the world I knew very little about. She helped me see beyond the veils and beyond the stories the western tabloids create to ultimately understand that we are all one. We didn't always agree on everything but we were both willing to explore with love and compassion and we worked out our differences through endless debates, creating theatre and letting each be who we needed to be.

We also got to travel to each other's countries and see each other's daily lives first-hand, rather than from past tales and photographs. This made all the difference in our friendship and in our creative partnership.

August 2005

The summer has gone so fast. Jacques and I have caught every ray of the sun's glow, we have played in every park, walked the Thames, watched films, worked together every night at the Old Vic, shared drunken kisses, made love in the theatre; he has whirled me into his poetic visions of words, writings and magical marvels of literature unknown to me. He is filled with tales from being on the road, of hitchhiking from Canada to Mexico.

I have invited him to move in with me and he is thinking about it. I hope he says yes! I am soon to travel to Jordan with Isha for a holiday and to do our show. It will be my first visit to the Middle East.

Jordan brought me new experiences in my search for freedom. I was there for a month in the dry, hot desert valley; the veiled women brought sadness to my eyes as they hid their true selves and ways. The mosques echoed their early morning prayers - with a sacred and healing mood moving over the city at five in the morning.

The feeling was so beautiful, so ancient and timeless. The

women are all covered with shawls, hiding their inner beauty. I felt that all their real truths, opinions, ideas and feelings were swept under another Koran and prayer mat. It left me with so many questions, questions I still think about when thinking about freedom – although today I see that it's not my place to change people, but to let them be, as they need to be.

I had the chance to see how difficult it was for Isha to be fully herself in her home country. In the Middle East it's all about honour and what's right for the family. One's true desires and soulful needs wash up on the shoreline of the Dead Sea and go unnoticed.

The notion that men and woman are equal in the Middle East seemed such an illusion to me. Women are covered up most of their lives; they can only reveal themselves to their husbands and children. Even in the modern day, women can't be seen with short tops or with skin showing shoulders and knees. It's one of the hottest places I have ever been; yet women are not permitted to wear shorts or skirts. My dressing routine was amusing: Isha's father gave me daily dressing inspections saying things like: "Samsunite, you can't leave the house like that, they will eat you alive."

This made my wardrobe selections very difficult.

I experienced a certain gaze from the men as though they were silently raping. It saddened me to realise that sexual restrictions and lack of equality between men and women had created such a complex, unhealthy and oppressive belief system.

My profound experience in Jordan renewed within me my search for sexual freedom, compassion, liberation, my passion for breaking down the systems that keep us in fear. I felt conflicted: on one hand I was exploring this beautiful country full of depth, ancient Sufism, family roots, rich languages, incredible art and abundant wisdom. On the other hand it felt difficult to be a woman who walks her freedom in a place where woman do not have the right to dress how they feel, travel where they need to go, swim in the sea, run in the streets or share their true beliefs.

I arrived back from Jordan to a very nervous Jacques. He was happy to see me, but something was not quite right and his unease made me imagine possible scenarios. Later in the week my suspicions were confirmed when he told me that not only had he had sex with one of the Spanish girls who worked with us, but also that he failed to use a condom. I flipped out and took us both for a sexual screening the following day. My anger subsided and I saw reflections of my own past actions playing out in front of me. It was a good taste of my own medicine. I wanted honesty and truth above all else, yet I still wasn't prepared to offer my full version of the truth.

My relationship with Jacques felt safe and when we were intimate I didn't feel any of the uncomfortable sensations around my breasts and sex. If I did I would tell him and he was always able to hold me in this space of feeling safe and held.

Jacques had an anarchic feel at times but his words were always filled with love. After he moved in with me things happened very quickly; his plans for Europe and travelling faded into the background and melted away. We got lost in each other. I still wanted my freedom; I wanted kisses from him and others and he didn't understand.

His jealousy moved inside me and I began a secret love game with the different people around me – I was noticing the surge of the energy of these attractions within me and wanted to explore and see what lay on the other side. I wished to be able to play each attraction out and yet still be committed to Jacques. This was not what he wanted and so I would let them go. Sometimes I would let alcohol-fuelled situations send my integrity out the window and have to explain myself the next day.

I was at the verge of the discovery I had been searching for, for years. I just didn't know how to play it out. I tried to recall conversations shared within Freedom Community, to explain to Jacques what I wanted, but when I spoke the words they did not feel like my own and he did not understand.

I wanted Jacques to understand my need to be with him and my simultaneous need to be able to explore with other people. He made me feel safe and loved and I didn't want to lose that. I also felt like I was able, for the first time, to be intimate with another and not have that feeling of rage and upset surface. But in my heart I also wanted to expand our love and let it grow to include other people. I wanted to be honest with him about it but we couldn't see eye-to-eye and this led inevitably to jealousy and tears.

I was looking for something, but what was it? "Freedom" was the word I kept focusing on, but what did this word mean in the context of my everyday life? Society says we can't have our cake and eat it, but that's exactly the freedom I wanted. I was yearning for it, I felt it at my fingertips – I wanted Jacques and I also wanted others. I wanted Jacques to share my bed at night and make love to me and yet I still longed for other experiences as well. I needed to fully embrace being honest; to fully choose the path I was walking.

September 2005

Sunny days stream in through my window and I am reminded of the heat of the desert and the beautiful travels to Jordan. Jacques and I are lovely. I can honestly eat him up at times, and yet all around me I see the attractions I keep with others. I need to make sense of them and see how to integrate them into my life. For the meantime, I am in bed with a beautiful man. He is curled up reading and I think I have fallen in love. It's amazing.

26 September 2005

Keep thinking, what is the point for us being together if he is leaving next year? I want so much more from him. I am beginning to see our differences and age gap as a problem. I also know that Love can arrive for a season to bring us into new ways of being.

I want to do more Landmark courses, and have also been thinking about doing a silent ten-day Vipassana retreat with a friend of mine, James. He is a Portuguese guy he is lovely, so artistic in all his ways. We have been in the same social circle for many years and he has also done the Landmark Forum.

September 2005

All these beautiful humans around me. I want to connect and touch their hearts. I believe our show will open up people's hearts to a new way of being tolerant, loving and compassionate, to a way of ending the world view that has invested so much time and money in war.

Creating and writing this show has brought me into full power; the process is magical. One day you have an idea, the next day you are playing improvisation in the kitchen; the first week the lounge is filled with material and newspapers as we find ways to tell this story and months later we have a show with sound, lighting, 15 characters and an audience.

I believe in evolving the human heart.

October 2005

The days are grey. Jacques stands so warm in his green suede jacket. So full of poetic knowledge. He is so beautiful like this, getting lost in his passion for Baudelaire or Henry Miller, or any of the other geniuses that have graced his life. I want so much more from him. I sometimes wish we had met later in life, once we have both touched the depths of what drives us.

His undefined boyhood sneaks through all the curves we take in our relationship. He has no responsibilities, no diaries, no real plans, yet so real for me in every way.

The world of the disconnected souls, running aimlessly, their heads stuck in the clouds of gossip, Drink, and Smoke, Jealousy, Envy and Sadness. My passion is to unlock the human love tank, to refuel hearts.

We need to walk in the veil of love and service for each other. Levels of depression are rising. More Prozac, more little white pills to help ease the overwhelming pain of self-sabotage.

We ignore the daily signs that would help us remember that we are divine vehicles of love; we block our hearts off from the angelic voices that would guide us to new, greener pastures of laughter, love-making, where we can dance naked every day in true celebration that we are all one. I truly believe that we are all interconnected.

October 2005

I believe we are here to evolve and push through all the boundaries, to find the freedom that connects us to all together like one amoeba cell.

I need to find the space to let Jacques be himself. I am finding a very warm space for James, my Portuguese friend. He has done the Landmark course and I am deeply grateful to be able to hold conversations on a deep level that both he and I understand. It's great to have this new-yet-old friend sail into my life. We met five years ago at a party and had this mad intense dance that cleared a full circle around us. We never exchanged numbers, yet he has always been around.

"Freedom" becomes a recurring theme from this point throughout these pages. What did it look like? The Freedom I was searching for was the freedom to love another intensely and lovingly while at the same time still being able to be close and intimate with others. The freedom to be my fullest self-expression without others judging or blaming me. The freedom to be naked among friends and not have it mean anything, to be able to cuddle and be close and sensual. To be with women, to share a space of acknowledgement of those close in my life and around me. Freedom from worrying what other people think. Freedom to walk my chosen path with compassion, courage and conviction. Freedom to have the courage to find out what had happened to me all those years ago in hospital.

26 October 2005

James is warming my heart; his tall bodily charm and blue eyes pierce my bubble. He is coming to the Halloween party. I wonder what he will wear. He always comes to parties in the most amazing outfits. First he was a parrot with an extra large beak who couldn't fit through my front door and then at our second magic mushroom party he was dressed as Marilyn Monroe with sneakers. He says very little but his energy is noticed. I think Jacques suspects my attraction to him. Something deep in me is stirring.

I could clearly see I was not built for monogamous relationships but I was still going through the very difficult process of accepting this about myself and negotiating the complexities of other people's attitudes about monogamy. It was through meeting James that I was finally able to accept the possibility of an open relationship.

I wasn't sure how long Jacques and I would last; I knew he was open, but not open enough to accept all I wanted with others. I would try and hold onto what we had and see how it all panned out; I was still very much in love. I also knew that the next relationship I stepped into would look very different: I would communicate very clearly before stepping deeper. What I wanted was a true open relationship

3 November 2005

Our worlds are so different; Jacques is a gypsy who believes in the suffering, the green little bottle of absinthe to find the

magic. His bohemian ideals are so captivating yet we meet on opposite sides of the same road. We come together in the moments of cuddling, being close, sharing movies, travel tales and making love. But the everyday of us is wearing thin. He does not believe in the spiritual path I talk of and that's OK. I believe in the differences we keep.

It all drops, I can't keep pretending, my kindred connection with my tall Portuguese artist friend, who I have known for many years, is playing itself out, and how convenient it is that Jacques is away. Our first unofficial date consists of non-alcoholic cocktails in Camden; he seems to speak my language of freedom, love, connectedness and community.

I wish to be with both of them, but I don't know what the tools to play this game are. The game of love I wish to create is showing up for me head-on and I don't know how to enrol those I love into their respective places in my heart. I don't want to play a silly love game but a game of honesty and integration. I don't know what to do with all this energy. I know I touch people in a way that has them experience a part of themselves that they wouldn't normally experience, sexually, emotionally or soulfully. It is all unknown territory that lies before me. I am terribly eager and nervous to find out

My relationship up to this point with James was much more a friendship. While Jacques was away we had the chance to hang out more and explore each other. We only made love a couple of times and he knew I was still very much in love with Jacques. When Jacques came back to London we continued loving each other and my relationship with James was still very present – it just wasn't in front of Jacques. We would hug and cuddle and kiss and that was mostly it. James and Jacques at this point had a strange friendship; they were connected by a woman they shared and who they cared for in different ways.

Towards the end of the year, I think Jacques was sad and hurt by what had happened. I don't blame him. I couldn't give him what he wanted and our beautiful love tale was becoming something else. We still loved and cared for each other in ways that overwhelmed us both. He was also younger than me and was looking for different things at the time.

5 December 2005

He won't say it because he's leaving, but I feel Jacques's frustration with James entering my life; and then when we kiss, all that melts away and we are back in the present moment of our love for each other. James and I have slept together a few times.

Next year I am going to see a therapist, the feelings have been coming up very strongly again. When I am with James I wish to be with him, naked, close and cuddled but not sexually. The other night I stayed over and spent the whole evening wishing to be with Jacques in our bed, the feeling of rage was the strongest it has been with anybody. I am not sure what is going on or what I should read into it. My body is definitely telling me something. My soul is fighting back and trying to open me up, something needs to be uncovered.

Jacques makes me feel safe for a number of reasons: his innocence, his ease with his sexuality, his love and tender touch for the female body and his vulnerability. The feeling of falling so sweetly in love also helped me just trust and flow the process and not feel so stirred up emotionally.

My rage around sexual intimacy began to surface again with James and it was the most intense feeling I had experienced up to that point. My soul was so connected with James, yet my physical body wanted Jacques and wanted to feel safe.

There was no chemistry between James and I, yet we had a spiritual chemistry that just got each other and I felt safe to share, talk deep and deconstruct the systems that we both felt kept people to think and stay in their boxes.

So, like many times before, when things got too much for me I headed home to the South African sun and to where my roots lie very deep – to a place that will always be home. Jacques decided to go back to Montreal so I was left with a bittersweet sadness in my heart at having to say goodbye to someone who touched my heart for a season in my life. A beautiful poet who understood my language for writing and fed my soul.

I knew I wanted to be in a relationship that transcended all barriers, gave me freedom to play, to kiss and to inspire people; I wanted someone to create children with, a relationship of open conversations about the life I believed in. The conversations of philosophy, compassion, integrity and above all the conversation of what it takes to be able to walk our individual path of Truth and Honesty in this lifetime.

Who am I? I am magical passion, manifested daily. Yes, that

is how I feel. I am not a passport, a bankcard, a utility bill or a name. Who I feel I am is magical passion, manifested daily. Now the question is to get others inspired in my game.

So the best way to create this was to create another Freedom Event and that was what I did. The event *Fantastical Voyages* was an amazing tantric exploration of creating fantasy linked with the rawness and beauty of nature. I had five friends come from the States, as well as other close friends from home. The intention for the weekend was to individually create and share our fantasies – these ranged from running around a fire like Indians, a nine-way full body massage and exploring sensuality through the five senses, being naked with each other in a space that had us all be authentic, be our true passionate selves. The universe also guided the event; none of us had watches, yet we all seemed to arrive in the right space at the right time to carry out each other's fantasies. It was a magical weekend surrounded by love and celebrated freedom.

This event was so inspiring for me as it allowed me to really live by the ideas and notions of truth and honesty at all times. It saw me connect with beautiful men and women.

New connections were made on a sober level and I discovered the power in dancing *The Five Rhythms*.

I had always been moving and dancing. I started ballet at the age of six and to find this medium of movement was a big turning point for me. It allowed me to be free in the dance, no set steps to follow, no high heel shoes, no drunken people bumping into me; being able to dance with others in a space where I feel safe and supported. It continues to be an integral part of my life, from which I draw much of my inspiration and workshop material. It also helped me to start the healing journey with my ankles, which were very badly hurt from the past; and it was around this time that I was thinking of returning to South Africa to have an operation on my ankles that would rebuild my ligaments by cutting the tendons from my knee.

Five Rhythms had a huge impact in my life. The experiences in the classes gave me an intense feeling of intimacy, without this intimacy needing go anywhere. I found a way to release my negative feelings about things and let go of them in the dance. Dancing and movement have always been deep for me; I feel totally present and in the moment when I dance, it is where I feel most alive and awake. To be able to share this passion with other people on the dance floor – people who love it as much as I do – was like finding another beautiful family of friends. *Five Rhythms* also helped me feel more grounded in London and anything I was feeling I would be able to take to the dance floor.

After returning to London, I was ready to let go of what did not serve me. I was joyful at the prospect of creating a sober and clear relationship, which would allow me to connect to the present moment: deeper intimacy to explore hidden parts of myself that I still didn't know, and to start to investigate my early years in hospital and how that had impacted me.

At the time I thought being single was the first step in my path towards creating an open relationship; I believed that as a single person I could choose who I wanted to play with and I didn't need to stay attached to anyone. I couldn't have been more wrong. What I really needed was to be in relationship with someone where I could devote and anchor myself, while being able to play and have other experiences.

March 2006

My sexual desire for James comes in waves; I feel one moment so in awe at what we can create, and then deep in our nakedness I wish to smash his head against the wall. As his hands outline my body I am filled with much trauma of my past. I can't ignore what is happening. Strange memories are coming to the surface. Strange smells of hospital are with me and I can begin to taste this flavour of rage and upset that has been with me all my years since opening up to this path of sexuality.

Night after night James sleeps next to me, his desire to touch me mounts as I ask him not to. His sexual journey is waiting to be explored and I am stopping his flow. We have a deep, loving connection. His patience astounds me. I know we are meant to create a family together and be together yet I just wish to not be sexual with him.

My childhood memories play over and over again as I begin to face up to the feelings that have been with me always but are only now pushing through to the surface. My days of being in hospital in plaster of Paris with my legs in splints have left deep hurts – I know I was abused during that time, I know I don't have to be all dramatic about it; I just want to come to the core of what happened. It all feels very blurry, like an old thirties movie. No sound, just slices of images and feelings that fill my body with a rage I can't ignore any longer. Who hurt me? What happened.?

Having James in my life is bringing all this stuff to the surface. I know that he has come into my life to show me my shadows that I cannot see on my own, and to guide me to begin to heal the scars that have been with me for so long.

Starting to walk this path of honesty and trust was bringing these past memories to light. I wasn't seeing a therapist at the time, but I knew somewhere in my search I would need to see someone who could help me process and integrate these feelings and memories into my everyday life. In the meantime James and I continued to carve out a beautiful dance. He allowed a part of me to come to rest - to find ease and to let me be me. I also found great healing in the dance itself, allowing my feelings to be moved through and not stay stagnant.

Stillness

Stillness is a place I have been searching for inside my busy head for years, months, days, hours and seconds. For most of my life I've felt like a wild stallion, always galloping my way through everything and unable to savour the sweet nectar and magical power of the present. I know stillness has always resided within me; she has always been there, I just never allowed her to come out. I never thought stillness would come in the form she did.

Stillness moves within and all around us. The dance is our vehicle, our destination is the rhythm of stillness and our challenge is to be a vessel that keeps moving and changing. Eventually we dissolve into meditation where all other rhythms of our journey converge in the vital resonance of stillness. Moving in stillness and being still in motion transforms our life experiences into wisdom.

In the past I have always held my breath and fast-forwarded

through the quiet times, created endless dramas and chaotic moments held in and held on. I wasn't fully breathing, so part of myself was locked up; I shied away from the ultimate teaching of life. Finding stillness has allowed me to fully engage with magical synchronicity and with the truth and quietness of my own mind.

In my deepest moments of fear and anger I can now reside in a still place: a place of inner calm where I can witness myself and not be swept away by the fury of the moment. In this place I am able to see the sacredness in all things. In my deep moments of motionlessness, I feel such immense gratitude for all that I have and all the beautiful souls I know and love.

My path with James in many ways has not always been easy; we have had to work hard to create chemistry and abundance. Yet his flow, openness and perseverance has anchored me and his gentle ways have helped guide the wild horse I am to green pastures. I had no idea that he would end up being my life partner, my best friend, my companion, my husband and the father of our children. James' beauty astounds me every day; his deep sense of calmness has grounded me, we keep expanding deeper and deeper into what it means to love another being. The love for Mother Earth, for the Universe, for the collective and for ourselves. There is so much truth in our connection; our relationship continues to expand through time, space, everything.

March 2006

VIPASSANA: 10 Days of Silence

Words do not capture the purity and clarity the silence gave me.

Each day my dreams, my waking life and my meditation rolled into one huge expansion of compassion and ease. I felt a cool blue liquid starting at the tip of my head, pouring a silvery blue light of stillness throughout my body. I feel a calmness I had only previously dreamt of. I know that I am not meant to perform for the next while. My healing talents and skills and channels are to be nourished and watered. I am to give myself to the silence, discipline and magic of living in the ever-changing world. "Everything arises and passes away." The divine map within me is opening.

One thing that was deeply clear in one of my meditations is that James is the one I am meant to have children with. I could see them clearly at different ages. They have his eyes.

I was slowly falling in love with James and in a very strange and unusual way. All the other men in my life had started from an attraction and sexual connection. This was all working the other way round. My soul was beating for him; I did not have the passion and heat with him sexually, yet I knew we were meant to be in each other's lives. I did not want to put any pressure on myself for not having sex with him.

It was around this time that I was able to speak to my parents about my suspicion that I had been abused, and how this was affecting my sexual life and my relationships. This allowed me to step a little deeper into my healing. My dad offered to pay for me to see a therapist who might be able to shed light on the situation. I decided to let every day reveal what it revealed and to trust what was happening, even if it felt uncomfortable and frightening.

My first healing sessions helped me feel lighter and it felt so valuable to be able to talk to someone about my feelings that in my head felt like such a contradiction. The memories are always the same and very blurred. A hospital, coldness, the smell of medicine, my legs in plaster and feelings of deep vulnerability and abandonment. I knew it was not one event, but happened repeatedly at night over a long period. As the sessions continued I felt a slow calmness beginning to dawn in my being. Things take time to heal; I felt proud of myself that I had been able to start to let it out and share it with someone who didn't know my past or me. It would take a another several years till I was able to really understand the full depth of this trauma and how it has actually been such a pearl for growth and wisdom and exploration into myself.

James and I had been together a long while and though we were not sexual we were creating a beautiful love container in which we could be our full selves. He held such patience with me around my sexual inquiry and he was able to let me be all that I needed to be in order to let myself heal and to be open and find my stillness.

It was July 2006, a week before my birthday, when a goddess from Austin, Texas, came knocking on my door. Her maternal love, her long wavy feather-braided hair, her angelic voice and her profound EFT healing tools helped me connect with being with a woman again.

EFT stands for Emotional Freedom Technique. It works on the meridians of the body on a very deep, cellular level, releasing old traumas and hurts and cleansing physical and emotional ailments from the body. One does this by simply tapping the meridian points of the face, hands and heart, along with saying affirmations such as: "Even though I feel this guilt, I deeply love and accept myself." I have experienced powerful results from this modality and it continues to be used in all my workshops and retreats.

It was so healing to connect closely with a woman again, she brought so much love into my life that summer in London. She showed me a version of what I wished to become and she radiated such a deep love and grace for humanity and the world. She gave me the best advice anyone had ever given me: she said I must go to the Rainbow Gathering – a free festival that happens all around the world, gathering communities to live, share and eat together in nature; it is centrally about reconnecting with Mother Earth, no drugs or alcohol allowed. She also told me to get myself to Burning Man. I followed both her suggestions and they created a whole new dimension of possibility in my life.

I left to America that summer without James. I needed to go by myself and see my community and experience living by the agreements that James and I had created for our relationship up until this point. They were: safe sex, no baggage, sober play and connectedness.

This may all sound vague or airy-fairy to someone who is new to the idea of open relationships. I know it did to me when I first heard about these concepts. I'll give you a personal account of my relationship with James and the agreements we have created in order to play this game of honesty:

We wanted to remain loyal to each other so we set up a safe-sex agreement so we could come back to each other in full integrity. James and I decided to have a relationship in which we would not use condoms, so any play outside our relationship would need to include very firm safe-sex practices.

No Baggage means that we don't get involved with others when this could potentially create drama; it means playing with people who are on the same page when it comes to wanting honesty and integrity in their lives. This is very important: there have been many men I had felt attracted to, but who were not prepared be honest with their partners or wives. They might say: "I am involved but let's just keep this a secret." I didn't want any secrets.

The No Baggage agreement really empowered me; it made me step into a new space of honesty with myself and for the other partners who were not present. It's a great feeling to give that level of respect to one's relationship and not just get carried away by a beautiful momentary connection that could create a huge ripple effect in the long run.

Sober Play is such an important agreement, and I loved to practise it. For me, it brings the first and second agreements together. You have seen that I have had a lot of sex with people when I was not sober, and this left shame in my body and damaged my self-esteem. Shame and I are now slowly becoming friends and just like guilt, I invite her in, to feel all her edges and all the uncomfortableness that goes alongside these two close companions. We have a chat and a cup of tea and then I ask them all to leave. This has become possible through my relationship with James as well as through my spiritual path.

I now choose to only be intimate with another person if we are both sober; this creates space for more intentional choices for everyone involved. It allows for safe sex to be practiced, it helps keep situations baggage-free and it allows one to really be present with the other person. In my experience, being under the influence can create a lack of authenticity and intimate connection. I have seen messy situations occur from drunken and drug-fuelled intimacy.

Connectedness means making sure there is a loving connection with new lovers rather than just a lustful engagement. This agreement stems from a very soulful place within all of us and it cemented my relationship with James. I choose to only become intimate with another if there is a true heart connection; if this new person is going to add something to my bond with James and ultimately strengthen it.

Being connected allows me to tap into the deep part of myself and to feel how I wish to play with the present attraction; maybe it's just a dinner or movies, maybe it is a long embrace and maybe it is something more intimate. The most important part of feeling connected is to know that I am choosing what this connection will look like and I am therefore being honest with myself about what I want.

The Burn

Burning Man is a unique arts festival that happens annually at the end of August. Sixty thousand people gather to build a city in the middle of the Nevada desert, Black Rock city. There is no currency used once you are in the festival (except to purchase ice and coffee and even then, if you don't have money, you can barter or even exchange gifts).

Burning Man is based on a gift economy; the currency you use is what you have to offer and this can range from art, massages, food, workshops, hugs or kisses. There is also a general agreement to give of oneself freely and not expect anything back. It is very beautiful to witness people giving so unreservedly.

Burning Man has a very strong "leave no trace" policy, which means you are responsible for your own rubbish and mess. No feathery things or glitter can be taken to the playa (the desert floor) because these can ruin the clay beds that have made it possible for the festival to happen here year after year.

Burning Man sees some of the best art in the world and people work passionately each year to bring their creations to fruition – these include everything from an eight story wooden structure that looks like a Belgian waffle to daily workshops on sacred mathematics.

Burning Man has a policy of radical inclusion. Nothing is forbidden, all is permitted. This allows people to express themselves freely without judgment or ridicule. There are always people riding around on bikes, being in touch with nature, enjoying nakedness in the sun; creating a living, breathing utopia complete with street names. There is a deep sense of community and oneness.

The Burn

My days on the playa transcend any other experience I have had. It's a sensory overload. Forty-five thousand people creating a living, breathing city in the middle of the Nevada desert, all running about in full expression of who they are. It is awesome.

Add no money, only a gift-giving economy and you get radical.

Turn on the heat with outrageous beautiful naked bodies following water trucks and you have wet and wild.

Cover yourselves with factor fifty and jump into the lush and juicy happening of fifty thousand people's creations: art, workshops, cuddling, bands, art cars, dance shows, fire spinners, crazy costumes, cycling mania – you get insanely busy.

Add thousands of luminous neon lights by night with blinkies and glow sticks and you get a fairy-lit wonderland.

Pump up the volume of each art car, dome and DJ box and you need earplugs.

Savour the sweet delights of sensual and sexual play and you have a kinky sweet lush desert of flowing love.

Throw in no judgment, no cynicism, manifestation and yes to all and you find yourself in a desert utopia for eight days with love and healing power moving you into each magically manifested moment of being.

This is the best Self Development Course I have ever taken.

It was like being born again, like when I gave my life to Jesus in my early teens. Only this time there was no God. We were all gods and goddess alike. We all have within us a magic to create what we want while we walk this earthly plane. I experienced giving myself to the pure life energy that connects us all and makes us whole. I allowed myself to travel into this new freedom and let it all flow, without guilt, without shame, without judgment and without fear.

Burning Man was the first time during this journey that I was able to really feel free for a long length of time. To be a part of community and all the beautiful souls I met was so dazzling; I had to remind myself that this was really happening, that I was creating this reality for myself.

I was able to be naked where and when I liked, I was able to cuddle and snuggle my friends without it having to be sexual and I was able to have really stimulating conversations about my feelings, my relationship with James and all other matters of life in a supportive and nourishing environment. I was also able to meet many other people and communities who successfully practise open and polyamorous relationships. It was so inspiring. I was like a sponge, soaking up all the learning, all the tools.

The Burn not only allowed me to find a new sense of my sexual self – it also helped me develop my healing powers and intuition. It was on the desert playa that I happened to meet two different women who had gone through the same operation I was going to have in South Africa in the coming month. Their results had been complicated and they still had serious problems with their ankles. They suggested I look into other methods before finally choosing surgery. After a long week of deep reflecting, prayer and angel guidance, I decided to enter the journey of healing my ankles though alternative medicine and methods.

At the end of the Burn, I phoned my parents at some ungodly hour in South Africa, cancelled my operation and my flight back and shared with them the alternative route I was about to embark upon. My dad's response was, "What, are you going to hug trees and heal your ankles?" I didn't even know where I was going or what my journey would look like; I just felt it deep within my heart that the decision was right. I was going to take the healing into my own hands. I was going to let the universe guide me.

I felt like a new me during the journey back to London, sitting in row twenty, gazing out the window with joy and celebration in my heart. I was on my way back to the arms of a beautiful man; I was tingling. I felt more grounded in my sexual nature. The healing was happening; the shame was lifting and I could let love flow through me with honesty and clarity.

In the month after I returned from the States, several things happened. A friend handed me a magical book called *The Shaman's Last Apprentice* by Rebekah Shaman. This book led me to discover the powerful healing properties of the Amazonian vine/tea Ayahuasca. This ancient Shamanic tea is a medicinal plant, used by shamans for healing people with physical ailments, addictions and emotional troubles and also for working with the consciousness. History has it that it was first used for guidance when hunting in the Amazon; it was said to enhance intuition and connection to surroundings. It has been used to discover the healing properties in many other plants and to see illness on a spiritual level.

I read the book twice within the following months. I knew there were ceremonies in London, yet I still felt rather hesitant. Then, a couple of months after Burning Man, a close friend told me about a beautiful musician and medicine man who works with the vine. I booked James and myself in for our first Ayahuasca ceremony.

Before one embarks on a ceremony, one needs to go through a process of cleansing both body and mind. The guidelines for this are not set in stone, and they vary from shaman to shaman, country to country. In our case, it involved fasting for the day of the ceremony. We were told to avoid all fermenting foods, sugar, alcohol, red meat, drugs, and to be sexually abstinent for a week before.

The journey itself was the most profound experience I have ever known. So intangible and not easy to put in words. The spirit of the plant moved deep within me and I was able to face myself completely for the first time. I felt as though I was experiencing a death – the death of my ego. At times it was dark, intense. I had to face my fears, to go deep within my physical body, into the cells and atoms that make up who I am. I had to surrender fully to the moment of just being and release the mind of being in charge. I was able to see the matrix of our grid that makes up this tapestry of lives. I was able see how past traumas can be carried with us again and again into our future canvas until we release them and find forgiveness.

Highly gifted musicians created the environment for the ceremony; the music guided and supported me along my journey. I felt a new lightness, a softening and a deep melting into letting go of all that I was and all that I thought I was. The peace at the end of that ceremony is like no other. As well as being an individual journey, it is also a collective healing ritual; the sense of togetherness, oneness and community was astounding.

During that first journey, I worked on my ankles; I saw how the injuries in my ankles were related to my lack of control and dishonesty in my later teenage years. She – the medicine spirit – showed me that the spiritual path I was walking was very much what the universe needs in order to heal herself and heal humanity. I felt the medicine working deeply within my ligaments and restoring them. I worked with my fears and the shame and guilt that still held energetically in my cells. I saw how my teenage years – as wild and amazing as they were – also left huge areas of damage and self-abuse within my cellular make-up.

A week after my first ceremony I was able to run seven kilometres. My ankles felt the strongest they had in years. I was able to maintain balance while standing on each leg separately. It felt miraculous. I felt aligned and whole and ready to put both feet firm on the ground and dance my dance.

This result has allowed me to keep following my path of movement as medicine. I have been able to continue deeper into my dancing practice, start teaching kundalini yoga and start my own movement practice called 'Body Choir', which draws from kundalini yoga, heart tantra and The Five Rhythms. Having my balance in my ankles has given me back responsibility for self. I continue a daily practice of reminding myself to let go, to keep surrendering to what is. This can be very challenging at times. We become too attached to our stories and the meanings we have put behind them. This path of awareness gave me an active role in continually releasing myself from the story, so life can move forward into each moment.

My first ceremony was by no means a complete fix. I have been working closely with the medicine for a number of years since, journeying deeper into myself in more ways than I can begin to write about. My ankles are also healing as a result of my new mindset, my daily meditation, yoga and not wearing high heel shoes.

The medicine is a space for people to come together in community, spirit and divine celebration of what is possible when we step closer to the light beings we are. The family I have met in these circles stays with me forever; it feels like we are one celestial tribe.

Since Burning Man and my first Ayahuasca Ceremony my world had shifted in many ways that still leave me spellbound. I went back to the Burning Man with James and we have grown deeply into our love. We had a magical wedding ceremony and our relationship continually shifts and shapes around who we are in each moment. Our love has brought two magical boys into the world, who we love dearly. It is such a special privilege to be parents, and that's a whole book in itself, for another time.

'Remember the entrance to the Sanctuary is inside you'

- Rumi

Our Open Relationship

My 12-year journey with James has been an extraordinary dance, all the other rhythms running simultaneously and dancing and weaving themselves together. James has allowed me the space to explore my attractions and not feel wrong for doing so. He has helped me release the shame and guilt I have felt in the past around promiscuity. It is amazing to have had a partner who is such a stand for my exploration and growth as a person.

Our open relationship allowed us to be with other men and women. I have been able to be close with old and new partners in a way that fulfils my needs. This is not just sexually: sometimes it's cuddling, hugging, kissing – sometimes just a coffee.

What we have found in our dance together is that when we share our attractions and our fantasies with each other, they dissolve into another passing moment and the energy disperses. I feel lies, lust and cheating all stem from the fact that we do not share what is occurring for us in the moment, and it builds and gathers momentum.

If we have shared the attraction with each other and it does not disperse, then there is something to open and explore. This is where James and I developed our relating, in learning to integrate these connections, to explore them and to allow all of them to happen within a safe open container.

Our love has seen us through many open roads, terrains, cobbled streets, dusty sidewalks, dark alleyways and crowded squares; along flowing rivers, rapids and waterfalls and tasting all the magical elements of nature that have greeted our path. We have had to learn to step out of our comfort zones into honesty, again and again and again. Though this has been challenging, it has brought about the most stimulating and enlightening conversations which have moved us deeper and deeper into who we are now and who we need to be in the future.

Our relationship has been filled with light and dark counterparts. We have navigated our way through upset, pain, betrayal, tears, fears, rejection and facing our lack of sexual chemistry for each other. Yet light always shines through the dark and we have dived deep into the tales of travel, honesty, communication, joy, wisdom, laughter, acknowledgement, gratitude, cuddling, affection and most important, being parents to two very special beings whom we both love and adore.

People and relationships have always fascinated me. All too often I see a pattern of fear in relationships. If we enter relationships with fear in our hearts that same fear manifests and can create very ugly games: the blaming game, the victim game, the past hurt game, the jealousy game, the affair game, the cheating game, the hitting game, the nasty words game, the "I'm right and you're wrong" game, the lying game, the giving up game. These games are powerful distractions that keep us from playing the one game that I believe we were meant to play: The Game of LOVE.

I believe that by choosing love we are choosing freedom. Most of us are governed by fears that overwhelm our journey to discover this place of freedom within love. If we break down the word FEAR – then all we get is False Evidence Appearing Real.

Within any game there are rules. In the Game of LOVE, a better word for "rules" is "agreements." The Game of LOVE is a lifetime of work; I still find myself tested and challenged daily. Having these agreements in place allows me to come back to myself and what is important to me.

For me, the Game of LOVE has three simple agreements. Once these are established and activated in our lives they begin a chain of events that push us closer and closer to our true inner purpose and our highest expression of personal being.

The Agreements

Honesty: Honesty can open up worlds of light inside our souls. When we are honest about our feelings, needs, actions and intentions, we can begin living in the light of truth. The energy change that takes place in our bodies when we withhold or twist truth is like cutting off our ability to fully breathe; many physical ailments manifest when we are not being honest with ourselves and others.

For me, dishonesty has manifested as physical anxiety. Looking back at the time when my dad discovered that money was missing, this made me sick inside. For months I collected fear-based energy and my body was going crazy; I was a time bomb waiting to explode: nervous all the time, worried and always sweating.

When I told my dad the truth that it was me who had stolen it, my shoulders and breathing immediately relaxed. It was game over. The truth was out and despite my father's anger and disappointment, letting go of the lie was the purest feeling of release. This was the point of departure in my journey towards truth, although it took many more struggles to reach the core of this pattern and to stop the lies once and for all.

Truth transforms us; it offers us new ways of seeing things and handling ourselves. It creates the possibility for our words to hold the power of real creation. Words have the power to unite us, yet we usually choose instead to let them divide us. Through my path of discovery, honesty has paved the way for deeper enquiry into communication and compassion. The Landmark Forum and Non-violent Communication have been pivotal works for allowing me to practice authentic communication. I am so grateful for these tools.

James and I took this Radical Truth into our dance; it has been our teacher in times of great opening and realisation.

Integrity: This is a concept I only began to understand a few years ago – the concept that our words are the commonality that imbues human interaction with meaning. Language is the anchor that makes this world real. Integrity allows us to be powerful beyond measure; we stick to our word and follow through with our commitments. This allows us to be in alignment with our needs and to honour our truth.

We are responsible for the words we speak and the words we don't speak. Integrity means being responsible and accountable for all that comes our way. Our words have powerful impact in our lives.

Integrity is the measuring stick I use to observe where I am holding back, where truth needs to be spoken, where commitments need to be honoured and where I can claim my most powerful centre. Every day I try to renew my integrity to the commitments I've made. Sometimes things happen and integrity flies out the window; when that happens it's OK – it's just important to acknowledge that integrity has been compromised and to keep trying.

I know this all too well from my days of drinking and taking drugs; I made promises and told lies, and I'd wake up later remembering the nonsense that I had spoken. This kept me from being reliable, and not being reliable kept me from being powerful. My intentions were good, but there was no solid foundation for those good intentions to grow on and become truth.

Integrity has allowed me to claim my power and to acknowledge my weaknesses. It has allowed me to grow into a leader and to develop the strength to be able to tell the truth. Ultimately, this has allowed me to start loving myself fully, truthfully and compassionately.

Choice: Choice is the result of speaking truthfully and honouring our needs with integrity. This means that we always have power in all that we take on in our lives. I had a choice to keep lying and cheating; instead I opened myself up to the game of honesty. Cheating and lying were nasty games; I was withholding and distorting truth just to protect myself from looking bad.

I lied because I wasn't ready to deal with the responsibilities in front of me; because of this, for many years, I felt like I didn't have any choices in my life. In fact I always had choice. I didn't have to feel guilt over my actions; I was choosing these actions to experience myself on all levels.

This can come down to the Law of Attraction: we reap what we sow. When it comes to the Universe and this game of life, we truly are masters of the blank canvas. We have the ability to choose whatever we wish, with a simple, "Yes, this serves me" or "No, this does not serve me".

This takes years of practice, but the sooner we realise that life is a choice, the sooner we can stop blaming others about the job we don't get, the guy who hurts us, the boss who doesn't pay us enough, the partners we keep fighting with, the jobs we don't go for, the actions we are too scared to take and the passions we never activate. Once we acknowledge we have choice, we can step into the world, take full responsibility for ourselves and know that we are in charge.

HONESTY is the first step towards being in alignment with our needs; it paves the way for us to be responsible for our words. INTEGRITY is our measuring stick; once we learn to use it, we can begin to make powerful choices. The CHOICES we then make can be honest and intentional, and we can finally play the creative game of becoming the masters of our lives.

Another amazing tool that I have learned from being open is Jealousy. Jealousy has become a great tool in investigating why I feel certain feelings and where in my body I am feeling them. In my relationship with James, jealousy has been a great tool to understand that what I am feeling is mine to hold. Though I may share and express what is coming up for me, it's not for me to project and make it someone else's problem. What I have discovered about jealousy is it can bring me back to the root, to the core wound within. It brings me to the wounded little girl who thinks she is not enough and feels like she is being abandoned. Learning to use jealousy as a mirror reflection of what is occurring within me has allowed me to move through some otherwise very challenging situations.

Here are four steps that I have used to investigate and navigate my jealousy. These steps can be applied in all relationships we keep, not just romantic ones.

Enquiry:

The more we can educate ourselves on managing our emotions within our relationships the better. I did a lot of reading and investigating and talking to other people about what jealousy looks like. All the reading and researching allowed me to realise I was not alone, that we all feel and can experience jealousy and that we don't have to feel wrong for feeling it.

Releasing Shame:

Identifying and owning our jealousy is the first step in dealing with shame. We have so much shame around feeling what we feel. To be in a space where we can own and share our feelings takes the shame away from feeling jealous. We can then give ourselves the permission to be jealous and feel into that space, no matter how uncomfortable it may be. Like all emotions, it's OK to be jealous, it's how we navigate it and move forward that determines our actions.

The Root:

In my relationship with James jealousy would come up from

time to time. It was most present for me when we used to dance The Five Rhythms practice together. We would be having the best dances with other people and then the rhythm of stillness would arrive. He might be having a beautiful dance with another woman and inside I would be going crazy with feelings of anger, rejection, not good enough. The strongest thought narrative that used to play in my head was, 'He will leave me'.

After years of playing with this dynamic I could see that all my jealousy takes me back to my years of being in hospital and feeling abandoned. Though this was not the truth, the feelings are real and are held by a little girl of one year old who just wants to sleep in her own bed at night, not in a hospital bed. A one year old who feels alone and abandoned.

Jealousy triggered by James was not because he was doing something "wrong," but because it brought up feelings from my past. By finding the root cause of my jealousy, I have been able to work on strengthening my relationships and myself.

Communicate:

Communication is the foundation of all the relationships we keep. The way we communicate is so important. Communication is about increasing understanding. If you simply say, 'You made me feel this' and leave it at that, the conversation is done, and you're not increasing understanding because your partner still has no idea why. I feel it's important to share with your partner what you are feeling, what it's bringing up within you, and to own it for yourself; to investigate the importance of communicating without blaming the other person.

One thing I have realised is that no one is responsible for making us happy. Only we can do that for ourselves. We can never expect something or someone else to fill that void. Over many years James and I have spent many nights talking long into the early hours, communicating, communicating and communicating. It is a very powerful tool.

"May your choices reflect your hopes"
- Nelson Mandela

Stepping Deeper

My traumas of the past continued into my long dance with James. Although there was a calmness and acceptance of what I had started to discover and heal about my days in hospital, I knew deep down that I was running away from myself. I was married to a man I was not attracted to. I loved him deeply on all other levels and although our open relationship meant that I was able to have sexual experiences with others, it didn't allow me to connect with one being and step deeper into that vulnerability and depth that I yearned for and needed in order to heal and release this trauma and pain.

Stepping Deeper into my truth and myself has been so humbling and has brought such profound change into all areas of my life. It has been the most confronting time and one that continues to take me to realms of the unknown that I did not realise one could reach.

Waking up is often hard, even when we feel we are on the right track. For years I felt that open and polyamorous relationships were the only right way to be. Looking back now I see how self-righteous I was in my many attempts to make this model of relating work for myself and those around me. I see how over the years my energy has leaked from the container as I looked for the right relationship and connection.

James and I towards the end of our relationship entered into uncharted waters of polyamory that neither of us were equipped to navigate. We had our agreements safely under our belts and with that we marched straight into the deep waters of the not knowing.

What I have learnt can hardly be put into words. I feel that Love in itself does not have agreements and when you fall in love so deeply it's not possible to rationalise or dictate its movements and flow. Love runs its own course. It has its own set of unique ways of being and it changes from constellation to constellation.

Around this time James and I had both met other people for whom we fell very deeply. We tried for a while to integrate all that was happening for us alongside our very precious and busy family life with two small boys. After five years of breastfeeding I was finally coming back to my body and feeling like a woman again. I was also still very confronted by the space of not being attracted to this amazing man I had married, and all the anxiety and overwhelming feelings that came along with it. I was feeling that something had to change; something on the horizon was pushing me further and further along this path of truth that I had chosen to walk.

So I let this boy walk into my life. Our meeting was no accident. I had called him in. He has been deep a catalyst for my growth and healing. I was not going to be able to stop the ride and flow of this wave, and how deeply it would crash me into unravelling, undoing, resetting, removing, rewiring and rewriting my book. The connection was the strongest force of sexual energy I had known. It took me into the deep shadowy waters of my own mind, fears, tapestry and the time all those years ago in hospital.

It has been an extraordinary and deeply revealing journey to be monogamous and present with one person after years of openness and playing the field. Seeing the magic of what can happen when one commits oneself to being with one partner has left me with many new insights and understandings. It also showed me how for years I had been running away from myself, not able to face that deep intimacy – Into Me I See.

Jacob has allowed me to meet a deep shadow part of myself. He has allowed me to really face the traumas of my past and to be able to meet the little girl within and start to give her healing and love. This has been the most eye opening experience I have embarked on and a true platform to explore my own wounded feminine and to understand what happened all those years ago – how it has been my fuel for seeking freedom and loving to love. The relationship took me over all uncharted waters of my being – it even took me to the Amazon Rainforest where I spent two weeks doing a silent diet with the medicine plants in Peru.

It was during one of the meditations in the Amazon that I was able to unlock the door to my years in hospital. Sometimes people come through to show you something and then when you have heard it, tasted, it, smelt it, felt and seen it, they go. This is that relationship. I am deeply grateful for all the murky waters that I have had to churn and go through with this dance, because finally I have been able to find the pearl, the truth, the narrative of what happened to me to many years ago.

So the story of the little girl in hospital looks like this:

There was a little girl who was born with her hips out of their sockets and at the age of one she was put into hospital. She had the most loving parents a girl could want, and each day she had a chorus-line of visitors and family playing and reading stories and photos reveal her as a very happy-go-lucky being. Yet as night would fall and the visitors and her parents went home to rest she was alone in a hospital ward, where her hips were tied up in plaster of Paris at a 90-degree angle.

As the lights would go out and she would cry, sometimes pillows were put over her face in order to muffle the sound, other times she was just left to cry alone with no warmth or human touch. She was left to urinate in her cast and not always changed. Staff mishandled her in horrible ways that no little girl should ever experience, and she would have to grapple with the notion of what it was to have her freedom taken away from her at such a young age.

Our lives are made up of a string of stories, each story telling a different tale and dictating the many junctions in our lives. What has been so healing is to own the story. This story I can now own, feel and let be. It's not the truth, it's not who I am, yet a part of my past that has shaped and lead me along this amazing course called life. By owning the past and understanding her messages, I get to rewrite the ending.

For me, the most important thing in my story has been how HONESTY has the power to transform lives. My journey has allowed me to discover the beautiful magic of telling the truth at all costs, of risking everything in order to live a free and honest life.

James and I are still closely part of each other's lives and we both see that our separation has been a blessing that we welcome. We are both walking deeper along our paths of truth, freedom and what the right relationship is for us individually and for our children. We continue to dance our dance as parents and friends.

Your beliefs become your thoughts
Your thoughts become your words
Your words become your actions
Your actions become your habits
Your habits become your values
Your values become your destiny
– Gandhi

The Dance

I believe it is time to start honouring our sexual selves by returning to our true Shakti (feminine) power: the qualities of love, nurturing, acceptance, heightened awareness, reflection, understanding, compassion, non-judgment, receptivity, innocence, playfulness, wonder, magic, celebration, beauty, harmony and peace. The essence of Shakti energy is in being, rather than doing.

Shiva, on the other hand, holds the masculine qualities of truth, action, facts, willingness, strength, commitment, dominance, persistence, protection, stability and determination. Shiva is the opposite of Shakti; the essence of Shiva is about doing, rather than being.

I feel that for too long this planet has seen Shakti and Shiva out of balance. For too long Shiva has been dominant, resulting in a humanity that is tired, depressed, angry, separated, joyless and afraid.

When we can live in a space of owning our sexuality – our own Shakti – then we can transform our sexual energy into a sacred and profoundly powerful tool.

Most of my past sexual endeavours have left me with burdens of shame. I've seen myself as promiscuous, unfaithful and sometimes I've found myself looking for love in the wrong places. These mistakes left guilt stamped on my heart. But when I look back on my one-night stands, threesomes, orgies, lovers, partners and colourful encounters, it is clear that all my experiences have been part of a perfect, magical tapestry.

It simply takes an act of willingness to bring us back into alignment with our tantric nature and our authentic self. I believe it is the energy of love that fuels our everyday moments of connection, our everyday memories. To love and accept ourselves completely is to open our hearts to the possibility of becoming whole; to know that there is nothing to be ashamed of and to understand that we are perfect in every moment of our lives. To see that even the most traumatic events can be the jewels and pearls of wisdom in the end.

There are many things that constitute a person's growth. My journey has had many side paths that led off the main road. There are so many stories to tell in each journey. My experiences have been influenced by all the travels I took as a teenager. Each trip out of South Africa grew my ability to see things with all my senses. Studying drama and becoming an actress allowed me to walk the path of self-discovery. Moving to London, one of the world's largest cosmopolitan cities, allowed me to dig deeper into my compassion and tolerance and discover the magic of dance. But among all the experiences that I have had, the ones that contain the most stories, the most life lessons, the most depth and the most explorations are my sexual journeys. Each relationship, encounter and partnership has led me to a deeper part of me.

Deep within our hearts we are all searching for ways to give and receive love. To open to love, to live our lives in freedom is our deepest calling. At our very core we are love and boundless freedom, and when we lose touch with this aspect of our being, we begin to yearn for that which is missing. The Feminine in each of us longs for deeper love and looks for it in intimate relationships, family and friends. The Masculine in each of us struggles for greater freedom and searches for it through financial, creative, travel or career challenges.

What I have grown to understand, witness and experience is that freedom, which is the flow of love, can be experienced and practiced through sex. Learning to have sex as an expression of our very being is like learning to play tennis or play the cello. You have good days and bad days. Sometimes making love is perfect, where body, mind and spirit are all one; other times it is scattered, anxious and with conflict. Even so, there is no such thing as failure, every moment is a learning, every closure an opportunity to learn how to live in love and open to love.

I believe that we are spiritual beings and we can choose to create the relationships that will help us express our joy to the fullest in this lifetime. The fact that some people feel unable to choose the relationships they want for themselves drives me to want to share my story and to work with others. It starts with loving ourselves and exploring what it looks like to create that right relationship with our own inner Masculine and Feminine.

Some of you reading this may be thinking, "I could never

have this". My point is not that you need to go out and create an open sexual relationship. This book is about you creating what you want for yourself; for you to reflect on your own experiences and to take a look at what it means to be truly honest and open with yourself and with those around you. There is not one way to have a relationship, yet what I feel is deeply lacking in our relationships is Honesty; in my opinion honesty is the key ingredient to making relationships work.

I have seen many monogamous relationship around me that are beautiful and appear strong, yet often the secrets and lies are so present underneath. This makes me feel there has to be another way to create our relationships. I have come to realise and accept that it is possible to love more than one person. Just as a mother loves her children equally and for different reasons, so does that translate into romantic relationships; yet we tend to make the assumption that one person will have to fit all the criteria to make us happy.

I don't have all the answers. Maybe for some having these secret stories or affairs gives a clearer sense of self; but I challenge this by asking, "Is there somewhere in your life you are lacking, not getting what you need?" I know that for me, now, polyamorous relationships don't work, I wish to be with one person and communicate openly and honestly. I never want to hold another back.

In my experience, withholding the truth makes energy stagnate; usually it means that another part of our lives is out of balance. The one thing that I know to be constant is change. Within that realm lies our truth. The truth is that our truth changes from moment to moment, just like change. If we can learn to walk alongside that dance, and be true to ourselves in each moment of life, then we can continue to transform like butterflies into our fullest potential.

An Open Relationship is a journey that I began to walk a long time ago; it's the story of how I learned to break down my masks, facades and lies. The journey to have an open relationship starts not with having multiple lovers and mistresses and affairs. It starts with living a life that is truthful in word, deed and spirit. It starts with understanding ourselves at a deep level which allows us to be lovingly honest and deliver our honesty with powerful and clear communication to all around us.

We let past experience dictate so much of what the future will be. We allow the hurts, rejections, suffering and stories to be carried forward into each new creation, each new moment. I believe we can move beyond this – by letting our past stay in the past: seeing it, being with it and making a choice to step into the future free of old wounds. Then we can create from a clean new canvas of joy and love.

We are powerful creatures full of needs, desires, passions, hurts, joys, sorrows, laughter and stories and, above all, love. It is the love deep within us that enables us to transform our relationships into brilliant sources of honesty, freedom and renewal: love for each other, love for ourselves, love for the universe and love for all the beauty within and around us.

We are divine beings. The Universe is waiting for us to start loving this game called life: our potential is to fly, to spread this joyous love all around our world. This planet is suffering due to lack of love. But love is always right here. In this very moment, as you read, I ask you to take a deep breath, draw your gaze from the page and close your eyes. Take a moment to be still, to feel gratitude for all that you are and all that you have in your life. Gratitude is the key for opening up the pool of love within; it allows us to see beauty within each moment. It is in these moments when life takes our breath away that we see the magic unity that connects us all.

I choose to live a life that is free, honest, full, unique, compassionate, sexy, celebrated, naked, raw, healthy, sensual, alive, evolving, teary, juicy and succulent. I choose a life full of travel, communication, dreams, manifestation, peace, wakefulness, compassion, reception, responsibility, knowledge, exercise, music, singing, ceremonies and joy. And above all, I choose to live a life that is full of unconditional love. What do you choose?

This book is my story of love. Love is all I know and it's all I wish to feel. Thank you for allowing me to share my journey with you. After years of exploring the person I am and was, I am entering my next cycle with love, truth and motherhood all around me. In order to move forward, I needed to let her story out. With this book I am entering my next phase of deeper self-love and awareness.

For me, the phases of life arrive in seven-year cycles; within the seven-year cycles there are individual years. Within the years there are seasons, and within the seasons there are months, weeks, days and hours. Within the hours there are minutes, and within the minutes come seconds, and with every second comes a moment. Each moment comes only once, so it is my aim to live in each moment as truly as I can to my heart's yearning.

Each moment is filled with the magic truth of love; this can transform us, heal the planet and bring peace to the world. Each moment comes with only one choice: love or fear. I choose love.

My final words

Many titles jumped out at me as I wrote this book; each month a new title presented itself until I landed on *An Open Relationship*. This title sums up how I feel – particularly if I take the word "open" and distil its essence to mean truth and honesty. By "relationship" I mean, how we relate to someone or something; in my life it is people I have related to most profoundly.

My life is about being in open relationship with those around me and most importantly with myself. I have chosen now to live my life honestly and therefore I have chosen to have an open relationship with all of you who read these pages. I choose to live openly always. The truth will always set us free.

All of the names in this book have been changed; each of these entries reflects the truth of a particular moment in my life. All the relationships I keep with those who have entered these pages are filled with honesty. No ties are broken.

To my Friends and Family I am deeply thankful to you all; to all who have crossed my path and helped me understand myself more deeply, thank you; to the bolt of thunder that has believed in me from the beginning – you know who you are. I am grateful. Thank you. I love you.

"One word frees us of all the weight and pain in life.
That word is Love."
~Sophocles~

~~~~~~~~~~~~

If you have enjoyed

An Open Relationship

please post your review on Amazon and

connect with me on Facebook

facebook.com/AnOpenRelationship

Or email me at Samantha@samantha-claire.com

With very great thanks,

Samantha.

ABOUT THE AUTHOR

Originally from Cape Town, South Africa, Samantha's background has been in the performing arts and dance. She has lived in London sixteen years, working in physical and ritual theatre on and off in the West End. Samantha is a Kundalini yoga teacher and the creator of Body Choir: an ecstatic movement meditation practice. She also hosts many holistic events in the UK and Europe.

Since the birth of her two sons, Samantha has worked in assisting births with her inspiration of natural home birthing. Samantha is a qualified Doula.

Samantha's love for life is the driving force behind her work and she is greatly inspired by The Five Rhythms, contact improvisation, Shamanism, Tantra, Kundalini Yoga and Meditation.

Her work is about recovering the balance and trust within our bodies, reconnecting to our heart centres, the source of our inner power and wisdom; and about awakening the freedom within, drawing elements from Emotional Freedom Technique, Vipassana, Landmark Education, Non-Violent

Communication and Shamanism.

Samantha's approach taps into a strong energy that allows people to connect more deeply to their mystical selves and to the vast, endless potential of love and compassion, which is inherent within all beings.

Made in the USA
Columbia, SC
22 May 2017